POP TODAY

Hamlyn

London New York Sydney Toronto

Editor and Designer
GAVIN PETRIE

Colour pictures supplied by London Features
International—
Cover—Noddy Holder, Sweet pages 24, 25; Slade
page 26; David Essex page 34; Suzi Quatro page 71;
David Cassidy page 74; Alvin Stardust page 98.
Other colour pictures: Donny Osmond page 23, Rod
Stewart page 73; Roy Wood page 111 by André
Csillag. David Bowie page 33 by Mick Rock; Elton
John page 47 by Chris Walter. Picture of Gary Glitter
page 48 courtesy Bell Records. Pictures of Queen
page 97 and Paul & Linda page 72 courtesty of Tony
Brainsby Publicity

Published by the Hamlyn Publishing Group Limited
London · New York · Sydney · Toronto
Astronaut House, Feltham, Middlesex, England
for IPC Specialist and Professional Press
© Copyright IPC Specialist and Professional Press 1974

ISBN 0600370801

Printed in Western Germany by Mohn-Gordon Ltd.

POP TODAY

Slade

By Rosalind Russell

SLADE, ace British slam-merchants, love touring in their home country, but it costs them a fortune. For every gig they play in Britain, they set aside at least £ 500 to pay for damage to the hall.

When they played at London's Earls Court in 1973, the total bill for damage came to £ 4000—and Noddy said he thought it was pretty good, considering the amount of people there.

"It's not wilful damage," he said. "It's just the kids standing on the seats and jumping about. They don't mean to break things. So we don't make any money out of our British tours. We have incredible expenses, and a road crew of about 12. The cost of hiring halls is going up all the time, so the ticket prices go up too, and there's not much that can be done about it."

However, it seems that although you have been paying more to see your favourite band, it doesn't stop you from spending even more money on them.

"I've been getting really amazing presents from fans," said Nod. "I've been given gold rings and watches. My parents have a lot of stuff in their house that's been sent."

And now, since their last American tour, the group have started to get gifts sent even from there, mostly just addressed to Noddy Holder, Spaghetti junction.

"Our records haven't taken off in the States, at all although the live concerts are great," says Noddy. We've headlined on the last three tours there, and have sold out on two of them.

"The thing is, our singles don't get any airplay at all. We can get our LPs played on FM, but the singles' station, AM, considers us too heavy. They're a more middle of the road station and play things like Dawn and Jack Jones. I think they're under the impression we're too raucous."

Noddy looks totally amazed that anyone could possibly think that.

"The kids have gone crazy at the shows, though. But then the next day we pick up the papers to read the reviews and they're terrible. The critics really don't like us. Even though we've had three encores and had everyone up on their feet, the reviews have said things like 'Slade failed to move the audience at all last night'. Sometimes you wonder if we were all at the same concert.

"They're a funny bunch, critics. We just don't bother to read the papers now, it doesn't upset us. We just go our own sweet way because that lot just baffle me."

Well, who needs reviews when you can sell as many records as Slade do. Their Xmas single sold a million copies in three weeks and was still top of the charts when the festive season was long dead. Within a couple of weeks of release, their album "Old, New, Borrowed and Blue" had sold 270 thousand copies—and that included the track that became their single "Everyday".

As soon as that went into the charts, they went into the Olympic studios again and set about recording another album. They don't hang about.

And so much for the people who said that Slade's style was such that they couldn't change it, and they'd never leave the stomping singles. Not only have they changed to suit their audiences, they have actually changed the audiences too.

There can't be many bands who have brought in such radical fashion changes as Slade. It's because it's such an event to go to a Slade concert that they hit on the idea of giving away prizes to the top Slade look-alikes.

The group's own appearance is slowly changing. Noddy gave up wearing his mirrored hat ages ago, although the fans still make them, and his general appearance has become rather more sober. Dave "H"

Hill is just as outrageous as ever, and still hasn't managed to lose much weight.

Both Jimmy Lea and Don Powell met old school friends they hadn't seen for years when they were touring Australia. It turned out that Jim's mate was selling jewellery, so he returned to England with a fistful of beautiful silver and amethyst rings.

"I've never worn much jewellery before," he said, displaying a glittering hand. "But I just couldn't resist these."

His pretty blonde wife wears only her engagement and wedding rings. Jimmy is the only married member of the group, and if the others have similar ventures in mind, they've been keeping very quiet about it. Dave does have a regular girlfriend, Janet, but they haven't mentioned marriage.

Slade have been regular visitors to the Disc Poll Awards, cleaning up in the Live Band and British Group Section rather successfully. As the event is always laced liberally with alcohol, Slade generally give it the proper party atmosphere. Once there was so much party spirit, they had difficulty in fulfilling the TV committment they had directly afterwards.

"We just kept looking at each other onstage and falling about laughing," said Dave.

Playing will always be fun to Slade, for when it stops being a laugh, they'll call a halt. It's practically impossible to predict how long a band's run will last, but when it comes down to it, everything depends on how well people in the band get on with each other.

Slade don't live in each other's pockets back home in Wolverhampton. Dave Hill lives a good way out of town, and has a house which directly overlooks a girls' school. His parents live more centrally, which is handy, because Dave's dad drives the group's Daimler.

Under the expert guidance of manager Chas Chandler, Slade go from strength to strength. Chas, to date, has engineered some of the best timing the music business has seen.

He has led Slade from obscurity to great success—one of the few managers who seems to be truly popular with his band. He is the man behind the planning of the tours and singles, and so far, he's been exactly right with everything.

Even with all this success, and the hit singles, it's only quite recently the band have started to acquire some of the trappings of stardom. The group have all been quite frugal, in comparison to their status, but now Lea, Noddy and Hill all have their own houses.

Noddy bought one fairly recently, with a garage housing three cars. Even so, to meet them you'd never guess that they'd had a sudden rush of money to the bank balance.

FLASHBACK: Slade in 1969—left to right: Dave Hill, Don Powell, Jimmy Lea, and Noddy Holder.

Sweet (left to right) Steve Priest, Brian Connolly, Mick Tucker and Andy Scott.

Sweet

By Rosalind Russell

THERE must be a lot of you out there who think that Sweet are the best thing that has happened since they put electric in the guitar. Despite a constant hammering from critics, they have grossed 14 million in record sales.

Taking a verbal hammering wouldn't be so painful—after all it's only words and the fans like them—but a physical hammering is something else again.

Brian Connolly, their aggressive lead singer with the bright blond hair, was attacked in Staines' High Street by a bunch of yobs and punched in the throat. The injury was aggravated by his refusal to take the proper amount of rest before starting rehearsals for their tour.

As his condition worsened, the tour had to be abandoned entirely. They took advantage of the lay-off to spend some time writing songs for the album. Their alliance with the Chinn/Chapman songwriting team had been a close one but for some time they decided to do a little rebelling of their own before returning to the winning partnership. They wanted to write their own songs—not because they don't like the writing of their mentors—but just to show people they can do it. In fact, much of Sweet's efforts seem to be taken up with trying to prove themselves. It's difficult to say exactly why they got themselves into this position in the first place.

They have always been aggressively protective about their abilities. Perhaps it was the infamous bummer concert they did at the Rainbow. So loud and proud were they before it, it must have been quite embarrassing to admit that the whole show had gone disastrously wrong.

They have atoned for that many times since. I've seen them turn in a couple of excellent shows; the lights were good, the music sound and the presentation well thought out. But people have long memories and the bad things tend to stick in the mind longer than the good.

"We'd have been lucky if they'd let us in to sweep out after that," said the band honestly. Perhaps that attitude at the beginning would have helped things along.

They took over their own management for a while, so that concert bookings would be in their own control. They wouldn't be pushed into going to the States at the wrong time.

"We want to rely more on our own writing talents," said Brian. "We still have Chinn/Chapman songs because they are good, but the proportion is smaller."

And surely this change of policy would also make for a different type of hit, because there was always the danger hanging over Sweet singles that one sounded pretty much like the ones before it.

"Not at all," said Brian. "You listen to them. Do you think Teenage Rampage sounds like Ballroom Blitz? The style of playing is the same, sure, but the songs are different."

Yes, but the change must be a welcome one, because there are some people who are a trifle bored by the same kind of hits appearing all the time.

"You are joking of course," said Brian. "We think the world of our fans and we would never cheat them in any

way by not giving them 100 per cent of our effort and talent."

And the fans do seem to get value for money. Now that their stage act is sorted out, it comes over as a smooth show. And it's long, running well over an hour. It takes in a wide variety of music, from soft rock to the screaming Ballroom Blitz hits.

And now they have the benefit of a really top class manager. After the dreary months of looking after their own affairs rather than trust them to someone they weren't totally happy with, they came across Ed Leffler.

He also manages the Osmonds, so his abilities speak for themselves. This valuable contact should open up many doors for the group in the States.

Before touring the States, they had to fit in a British tour to replace the one that was cancelled. Other commitments which were blown out at the same time had to find a place in the queue as well. Obviously, it was worth their while hanging out for the very best in management.

Time will tell how well their own songs stand up to their earlier hits on track record. Chinn/Chapman have a fair head start, but if Sweet are worth their salt, they'll catch up.

Alice Cooper

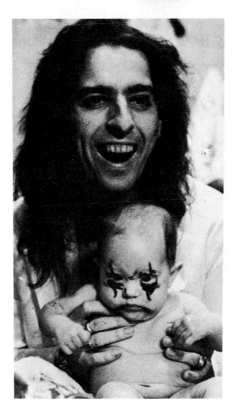

By Andy Blackford

ALICE COOPER has shocked and outraged his way across the world, blazing a trail of artificial blood, ritual mock-murder and phony executions.

Questions have been asked in Parliament: Should this monster be allowed to impose his sick soul upon the innocent youth of Britain? Should we permit him to deprave and corrupt our children with his bizarre circus of sadism and ultra-violence?

Even his own mother has to admit, "He's always been a little . . . odd." But what's he *really* like? What does he do when the crowds file out, the house lights go up and they start wiping the tomato ketchup off the gallows?

"They've got me all wrong," he complains. "Just because I cut the heads off dolls, they say I must hate babies. But it's not true. I just hate dolls.

"What I do isn't sick. Nor is it serious. It's simply entertainment. I'm sure it doesn't warp people, watching me.

"I sit and watch sex and violence all day—that's all you get on TV. It's what America is all about. Our culture's so young, there's nothing else.

Yet off stage I wouldn't harm a fly. I'm the gentlest person alive.''

When Alice claims to watch TV all day, it's hardly an exaggeration. ''It's true. I'm a real media-freak. I've just bought the world's largest television. It's got a screen four feet square, and there's a device which enables me to play back video-tapes of old movies. My manager's got over three hundred cassettes of old films from the Marx Brothers to James Bond.

''Even when I'm in bed, I still like to watch the late shows. I've got a special little portable set with an ear-plug for the sound. It usually go to sleep with it turned on—and TV in the States goes on twenty-four hours a day. So deep in my subconscious, I must have the sound-tracks to hundreds of movies I've never seen!''

Alice's other great passion is golf. He plays with Bob Hope when he's at home, and Carl Palmer when he's in this country.

It's the only thing that can make me lose my temper. Like the other day—I broke five clubs against a tree, just out of sheer frustration . . . ''At first the older players used to be a bit suspicious because of who I am and what they thought I stood for. But once you out-drive them on the first hole the chips are down, you're another player and it's a grim battle to the death.

''Besides, back home they have public courses as well as private clubs. I play on the public ones. There might be a few objections from the older members if I tried to join a top rank respectable club.''

Even so, golf is hardly what you'd expect a ghoul's hobby to be. Perhaps we *have* got him all wrong. But wait! You say you're writing a book, Mr. Cooper? Now that's more like it! It must surely be called *The Beast From The Black Marsh*, or *Son Of Frankenstein Meets The Thing From Beyond The Grave*?

''It's called The Adventures Of Maurice Escargot. It's about this amateur French detective who solves all the crimes that baffle the regular police. You know the sort of thing: 'Ah, alors, sacre bleu! We are, ow you zay, stumped. Thees eez a job for Escargot!'

''It don't get much time to write, but I bash out a page whenever I can.'' So much for Alice's book. No support there for the *Monster Theory*. Just a light-hearted detective story. No sign of zombies, Oriental sadists and de-composing corpses. Disappointing, really . . .

Still, there's hope yet. He's landed a part in a TV film. A remake of the *Corridors Of Blood*, perhaps?

''It's one of a series of detective thrillers called the Snoop Sisters. You have it over here, I'm told. It's about two dear, little old ladies who go round cracking murders.

''I play a witch . . .'' (hooray!) ''. . . but I'm not really a witch at all . . .'' (booo!) ''. . . I'm a con-man who's just making a lot of money out of pretending to be evil.'' (Perhaps that's a clue on our quest for the real Alice Cooper?)

''But haven't you noticed my change of image? I'm going romantic. It's the new me!''

True, now he mentions it, he does look distinctly clean-cut. He's wearing the American college kid's uniform of track shoes, faded Levis and white, short-sleeved sweat shirt. The only hint of the old Alice is a small badge sewn on his chest which reads 'The Queen Of Acapulco'.

The hair, too—shorter than we've seen it before, and layered. The over-all effect is one of careful casualness.

''Next I'm growing a pencil moustache like Errol Flynn's. Can't you see me, sliding down the rigging, cutlass between teeth, dashing to the rescue of some damsel in distress?

''I'm even taking fencing lessons. Two hours a day while I'm at home. I'm serious about this—I'd love to play the romantic pirate captain in a movie about the Spanish Main. That appeals to me.''

This is too much to bear. Why, only yesterday, a friend who used to work for his record company was telling me about the time the last train from Birmingham to London broke down miles from anywhere. And Alice disembarked and marched three miles along the track to a tiny country station. Hearing the sound of approach-ing footsteps out there in the night, the station master held his lantern high—and saw this hideous apparition in full make-up, a python en-twined about his neck. Needless to say, the poor official sprang half out of his skin and pelted, screaming blue murder in to the darkness.

And now we're expected to think of him as a latter-day Errol Flynn. Still—at least we'll still be able to believe in his sex-appeal. Errol, as well as Alice, was a great one for the ladies. Surely he must have whole ha-rems of wenches, chained up in sleazy cellars, enslaved to his every whim?

''Nobody can be *completely* good on the road. It's more than any man could take. But I'm pretty faithful. I've been going out with Cindy now for six years. It's a wonderful relationship.'' (How boring. Another illusion gone).

''She's a model, very successful. She has her own friends, her own so-cial life. She hates my show. Wild horses wouldn't drag her along to watch it.

''In fact, we've got nothing in com-mon whatsoever. Except we both think marriage is the world's most stupid institution.''

The only aspect of Alice which is true of Cooper seems to be his legen-dary love of things alcoholic. It was two o'clock in the afternoon when I visited him in his hotel. Already there was a pile of empty beer bottles on the floor which would have done credit to the Australian rugby team.

''I used to have a serious drink problem. I got through two bottles of Seagram's whisky a day.

''But I made a big effort, and now I don't drink spirits until after ten at night.

''I don't get drunk on this stuff.'' (Gestures with bottle). ''It just relaxes me. Sometimes I'll even go to sleep holding one of these. Cindy says it's a job to prise my fingers off the neck.

''I'm a terrible man!''

Not at all, Mr Cooper, not at all. You're Mr Nice Guy underneath the war paint. If they ever run out of the stuff records are made of, you could make a good living as a chartered ac-countant!

Playing it straight (right) The Alice Cooper band.

Rod Stewart

By Rosalind Russell

YOU COULDN'T call Rod Stewart good-looking. Not really. On his own admission he has a nose that's too big for his face, and that haircut can only be described as "extreme".

Of all the hundreds who have had their hairdresser do the same to their heads, Rod Stewart is the only one it's ever done anything for. He does, however, possess a pair of legs of undeniable beauty.

He rolled his trouser legs up in the pub to let us have a look. " Ace footballers' legs," he commented, with great satisfaction. He's as thin as a pipe and he sings with his shoulders hunched up around his ears. And he has one of the most distinctive voices that ever blistered the walls of any of our concert halls.

Stewart is probably among the richest of Britain's rock and roll stars, although he won't admit to being a millionaire. "I have the old fashioned idea of a millionaire actually having a million pounds to hand," he says.

But of course if you take into account his 32-roomed mansion outside Windsor, and his cars—a Rolls, a Lambourghini and a Mercedes among them—it could be that he could realise a million quid.

"I can't understand people who begrudge you having a lot of money," said Rod. "They don't realise the work you put in and the chances you've taken. If you'd failed, you'd have been left with nothing. But all the good people win in the end. Talent always comes through in the end you know. There's no point in someone saying that people in factories and mines get very little so it's not fair that people in the music business shouldn't be able to earn what they do. It's a question of the talents you have. What I do, no once else can. What you do, no one else can."

Apart from the obvious physical comforts Rod's money has brought him, he remains the same person underneath it all. He still gets a clip on the ear from his dad if he's caught sitting in his chair; kids that wander up the driveway of the Stewart mansion are generally treated kindly.

I think it's the mainstay of the Faces' success that they've stayed so close to their fans. Their stage show is designed to pull in the audience, to make them feel part of what's happening.

For a while the show looked very much as if it was going to be Rod Stewart and his backing band, the Faces, but only on record, because Rod still had to fulfil all his solo contracts. Now they are through—he has finished his last solo album—so we can all rest easy, knowing that they will be continuing full strength as a unit.

Mercury and Warner Brothers have finally sorted out all the contractural problems, which puts an end to the speculation, public and private, about Rod leaving the Faces.

However, it doesn't put an end to any other kind of rumour. Stewart, being hot property, is the target of many stories. It's embarrassing to read some of the stuff written about him; he is a human being after all, if only just a little larger than life. But then it is hard to write about a guy who is so likeable without getting all pedantic about it.

"I don't think you can ever over-expose yourself through playing," says Rod, "as long as you have the confidence to go to the United States or Europe. But the Press is another thing. Even I get sick sometimes of seeing my face in the papers."

Being a rock and roll star was only second choice to him—everyone knows his first love was football. So why did he start singing?

"It was the only thing I enjoyed doing, that I got paid for, without taking a regular job."

Did he ever think about a future without the Faces? "I need them. I could always make my own albums, but I'd be lost without them. I get depressed when I don't see the boys for a while. But I want to retire at the top. In this business, people tend to hang on, sinking lower and lower. I want to just disappear."

It's almost impossible to think of Rod just disappearing . . . he's too flamboyant, too much of an extrovert just to vanish. Even the simplest thing, like going out to a pub for a quiet drink, results in a public occasion.

The girl behind the bar is overcome with shyness and the couple sitting opposite sit and stare, too tongue – tied even to ask for an autograph until we are leaving. Stewart's charm lets him get away with murder.

During a Faces' tour of the States, Stewart carried a gigantic Scottish flag—the lion rampant—around with him. (He generally brings it out onstage at concerts too).

At every hotel they went to, Rod hung the flag from his hotel window—and sometimes it outshone the hotel sign in size. His preoccupation with Scotland and all things Celtic is well known.

And most Scots are just a little bit proud that he should want so badly to be thought a Scotia-phile. But most of this interest stems from the fact that he'd liked to have played football for Scotland. He and his brother used to travel up to Scotland for all the big matches.

Like his mate Elton John, he likes to get a game in whenever possible—usually at the weekends, but the venue is kept a secret—or as secret as anything he does could ever be. Possibly the only objection he has to being on the road is not being able to play. Well, that and the conditions bands have to live under doing British tours.

"The sad thing about touring over here compared to America is that British promoters are so penny-pinching. You do an American venue and it's all laid on in the dressing room. There are drinks in a freezer, food and maybe even flowers. Here, you're lucky to get a cup of tea and a sink."

When I saw them last, they didn't even get the tea. But then, the Faces have learnt a lot, so they carry all their own booze with them. And that's just as well. Once, when they were due to play at a theatre in London, the Who had been there the night before and decided to clean out the bar, just for a laugh, to make sure the Faces stayed dry.

The whole group refute the suggestion that they have to have a few drinks before they go onstage; they usually just have a couple. And it was interesting to note that while the generous Mr S was buying the drinks, he only had one to everyone else's two.

Osmonds

Marie

**From Jean Lewis
Hollywood Editor
16 Magazine**

Jimmy

OSMANIA! It all started in a small town in Utah in 1944, when a young lady named Olive Davis married George Osmond. Today, they are known the world-over as the parents of those super-talented Osmond Brothers, and pretty, equally talented sister Marie. All told there are nine children.

The Osmonds wanted a large family, and their first son Virl was born in December. Two years later there was another son Tommy, and then, one after another, five more sons were added to the family.

Alan (born June 22, 1949), Wayne (born August 28, 1951), Merrill (born April 30, 1953), Jay (born March 2, 1955), and Donny (born December 9, 1957).

On October 13, 1959, the all-male dominance in the Osmond household came to an end with the birth of the first and only girl—Olive Marie.

All showed an early interest in music and being a warm and close family, the parents naturally encouraged them. Every week, one night was put aside for entertainment, and everyone took turns. Mrs. Osmond played the saxophone and Mr. Osmond sang, and soon Alan, Wayne, Merrill and Jay were not only singing alone, but began singing together.

At first they sang just for the family and their own pleasure, but eventually word got around and they were asked to sing for a church luncheon.

Next came a trip to California to perform for the various church wards—the Osmonds are members of the Church of Jesus Christ of the Latter-Day Saints. The boys were more excited at the prospect of visiting Disneyland than performing, and after they'd ridden all the rides—many of them several times—they stopped to listen to a barber shop quartet.

Soon Alan, Wayne, Merrill and Jay began singing along and were invited to join the quartet on-stage. The man in charge of Disneyland entertainment was called and he hired them to perform at Disneyland all summer.

And so it was, that the Osmonds returned to California a few weeks later and Alan, Wayne, Merrill and Jay began their professional careers.

During this time, they also appeared on a Walt Disney television show and from this they received a call to audition for Andy Williams. Andy liked what he heard and saw, and scheduled them for his first television show and signed them as regulars for the next four years. That was 1962.

By 1963, all sorts of wonderful things were happening for the Osmonds. Another boy, James Arthur was born April 16. According to his brothers, little Jimmy even cried in-tune!

Along with being regulars on *The Andy Williams Show*, Alan, Wayne, Merrill and Jay, and actor Kurt Russell co-starred in another series called *The Travels of Jamie McPheeters*, and they loved it cos they got to act as well as sing.

Five year old Donny had been busy ''learning'' as he watched his brothers from the sideline, and when they got a call for another television special *The Seven Little Foys*, Donny went along and got a chance to sing and act and dance too.

Soon Donny was joining his four big brothers from time to time on the *Andy Williams Show*, just the way little Jimmy started later.

In 1966—after the Andy Williams Show went off tv—the Osmonds became regulars on *The Jerry Lewis Show*, and that's when Donny finally became an ''official'' member of the group. He was nine years old.

Next came numerous guest appearances on other television variety shows, combined with concert appearances with such stars as Andy Williams, Pat Boone, Nancy Sinatra

Donny and Alan

Jr., and Phyllis Diller. It was also the time for travel to such far-away places as Japan and Sweden, where they discovered they were loved, not just in the United States, but the world over.

In 1969, Andy Williams had another television series, and again the Osmond Brothers were featured. When the show ended after a year, they signed with MGM Records and recorded their first hit single *"One Bad Apple"*.

Television had been good to the Osmonds and 1971 found them starring—with little brother Jimmy—in their own special *The Osmond Brothers Show—He's My Brother*.

Each year their popularity increases. Everywhere they go, the crowds follow them and crush close to say "hello" and *touch*. Donny is the *favourite* target, and he's constantly teased by his brothers about the volumes of mail he receives from girls.

They've performed for the Queen of England, to sold-out audiences in Las Vegas and concerts in cities across the United States and around the world.

Their records are constantly played and are always at the top of the music charts.

And then sister Marie has her own hit, *"Paper Roses."* She smiles as she remembers her professional debut with her brothers in 1973 at Caesar's Palace in Las Vegas.

"It was a terrifying experience. I kept thinking that I might do something to embarrass them. I've never been so scared in my life!"

That, of course, did not happen, and Marie was a hit with the audiences and critics—and an even bigger hit with her brothers.

Alan beamed as he explained: "She was a real trouper. We'd been doing this so long that it was automatic. And when we began, if we made mistakes there were few people around to notice. But Marie started before huge audiences, and she was fantastic!"

Such family pride is the rule. And when Perry Como asked for Donny and Marie to join him on his television special in the spring, 1974, the rest of the family sat back and applauded.

Donny confessed that it was kind of strange not to be traveling in a "crowd" when he arrived at the studio

for the first day's rehearsal. And Marie added that "we only have our own suitcases. Usually we travel with more than 20 bags and trunks and it takes forever to get them from the baggage people and loaded into a van."

The Osmonds are a family not only devoted to helping each other, but have established a foundation to help others.

Its beginnings have a very personal cause. The eldest Osmond brothers, Virl and Tommy, were born with severe hearing losses, and when their mother ignored proven methods of working with deaf children to successfully educate her sons, she vowed that she would do as much as she could for others with hearing problems.

So with the continuing success of the Osmonds, they have continued their mother's promise through the establishment of the non-profit-making Osmond Foundation, which provides encouragement and the means and equipment needed to educate deaf and blind children.

The Osmonds not only sing from the heart, but they also put a song in the heart of others.

David
Bowie

By Fox-Cumming

THE HAMMERSMITH "ODEON", London, late summer of 1973—David Bowie: "This is the last concert we shall play—ever."

A Kensington hotel two days later: "Well the last one for a good two or three years anyway."

The music press, spring 1974: "Bowie set for US tour."

Bowie's former security guard, Stuart George, at around the same time: "It wasn't Bowie who made the

decision to quit. It was his manager Tony De Fries. At first David didn't want to do it."

The only certain thing you can say about Bowie's retirement is that it was short-lived. Who willed it and for what reason will now probably always remain a matter for conjecture. Perhaps he just wanted a rest from touring and if so, why didn't he just say so. By the way the whole thing was handled, he came dangerously close to blowing his career altogether.

How much longer the public would have put up with an absent star who put out single after single off old albums is anybody's guess, but there's a limit to even the most devoted fan's patience.

Bowie himself seems to thrive on creating as much confusion about him as he can. His public relations people must be the most ill-informed in the business. He tells them one thing and does another and the whole thing's quite deliberate. "It keeps them off the streets," he says. "Keeps them busy and keeps them interested."

He also quite unashamedly feeds the musical press successions of contradictory statements and isn't at all put out when the discrepancies are pointed out to him.

Before he "retired" in 1973, he told me: "One of these days I shall want to call a halt, but there's no way that I shall do so never to get up on a stage again." That statement proved both prophetic and accurate, but some months later while he was hard at work recording in Olympic Studios, he said: "I love it here. I think I'd be quite happy to stay in here forever and never go out on the road again." Two months later he was out in America getting ready for his "Diamond Dogs" tour.

His output during those six months in the studios was phenomenal. Enough material for at least three albums of his own; an album for the Astronettes and several tracks for Lulu.

On its own that may not seem too hefty a workload, but at the same time he managed to polish off scripts for two musicals and get various other lesser projects underway, including a film of "Octobriana" about the Russian underground press's comic strip heroine.

His energy is boundless. His wife Angie says: "Anyone who hadn't the

same energy level would find it impossible to keep up with him, but luckily I'm made the same way.''

Angie's main worry is that David won't eat. As Ian Hunter points out in his book "Diary Of A Rock 'n' Roll Star", "David's the only star I know who regularly suffers from malnutrition."

During the months that he virtually lived in the studios, getting up lunchtime, going straight there and working through until near breakfast time the following day, he would happily sustain himself just on interminable cups of coffee and packet after packet of French cigarettes.

Meals were cooked for him at home and sent down to him at the studios but usually after only a couple of mouthfuls he'd push them aside.

Sometimes this un-nutritious diet begins to take its toll on his health. He's collapsed on several occasions during tours. "But never," he says, "onstage", though once he did pass out right at the end of, appropriately, *Rock And Roll Suicide*". Most people thought at the time that it was part of the act.

Bowie's future is not very predictable. Sometimes he complains that he finds working within the confines of rock and roll too restricting, although he has managed to do so with spectacular success up to now.

However there's no secret made of the fact that he'd dearly love to graduate from being a pop star into more of a broader-based entertainer in the way that his old hero Anthony Newley did in the early sixties. There have

been mumblings in his organisation about moving on to greater things.

But Bowie's far too canny to take risks by moving too fast and, as he's still only in his mid-twenties, time is on his side. There's no desperate hurry.

He's spent more time satisfying his own ego. While he was enjoying huge success in Britain with up to five albums in the charts at the same time, people were not slow to point out that he hadn't really made it in America. Hence the concentration on the American market with the "Diamond Dogs" tour.

Once, as a rock star, Bowie has the whole world at his feet, then we can expect to see him looking for new avenues to explore. In the meantime, the music's still pretty good, isn't it?

David Essex

HE'S DARK, handsome and thoroughly enigmatic. He looks like every man wishes he looked and like every girl wishes he did. Looking at David Essex can be positively therapeutic.

The mystery behind the flashing light in his steel-blue eyes is every bit as deep as the one which lifted him from London's bite-and-scratch East End to lofty stardom both in Britain and the fast-paced, nervous U.S. of A.

He says little, suggests a lot. Avoids people, yet attracts crowds. Plays the loser, but triumphs by his very nature. Somehow, suave sophistication will follow him all the days of his life, and his cup will runneth over and over again. Talent exudes in his deeds on screen and in song. Everything David Essex does, simply radiates style.

By Lon Goddard

But wait—this seemingly temperamental genius, this apparently affluent, virile hunk of man, that guy with the endearing smile of an innocent puppy and the intense features of a young Alan Bates . . . lives happily in his Essex home with a wife, and kid and a dog—just like anybody else! He even wears jeans and digs the garden! Maybe there's more to this than meets the camera.

"I'm just casually looking good," says David about his appearance. "Unconventional, but comfortable. Trousers and even Y-fronts. Sweatshirts, jeans and a mean line in socks. I've even been known to wash!"

A distinct line in friendly sarcasm.

"I'm not really meticulous, but I don't smell. I like Aqua De Selva (please send the BIG bottle) and Eau Savage. I hate ties—I don't think I've ever worn one. I get up in the morning and brush my hair once, and that's all—I don't pay much attention to it."

Maybe it's the incredibly choice selection of clothes that make the man. Those nifty white suits and casually open shirts suggest a playboy Clark Gable lurking inside.

"I do have a big wardrobe, but I wear-out stuff fast." He is not wearing socks. "People are always telling me what to do—I just keep it in mind if it suits me, or I don't bother at all. White and blue suit me, black's O.K., but no greens or anything like that.

"I always wear flat shoes. I'd feel like an old tart in heels—I'm five eleven, so I haven't got any height worries. I wear an earring, because

there were Gypsies on my mother's side.

"I have periods of dress. Phases. I wouldn't follow trends, but I appreciate it when other people adopt my image—earring, baggy trousers and so on."

Baggy trousers and whatever, it's strangely reminiscent of a story as mysterious as the boy next door. If David shines bigger than life, the external additions only embellish his person. Must be something further down. Something we have to dig for, buried in his upbringing. He brings it up.

"I'm not a trendy fabster. There was never any rock or theatre history in the Cook family (he was christened David Cook). Only the docks, where my dad and all his brothers were.

"I was an only child. I never heard of a late night. I'd wake up, get up and go back to bed, have a cup of tea and some toast, then try to wake up sensible. My mum wanted me to be an engineer, possibly because my cousin was. I tried it for three months, but quit to become a professional musician.

"All my teachers in school thought I was a lunatic. 'He's not interested in his lessons'. Was that my fault or theirs? They probably weren't, either, but some did try. In that environment, there was either football, rock or violence—they were the only means of escape.

"I was pretty good at English and football (he made the West Ham Schoolboys team), but I escaped through rock. How can you get on academically when the schools are so rough and the teachers are the dregs? They wanted out, too!

"We were the only English family in a cul-de-sac. On Saturday evenings, the Greeks threw bottles at the Cypriots, Whites threw chairs through Blacks' windows—there were fights all over the place. It was so dramatic, it was commonplace. I just stood in a corner one day, and my mind went. I had to get out."

The street was somebody else's turf. The playground was a bombsite. The school was dangerous and hardly a source of inspiration. Most kids who grew up there are still there, but David is not. Perseverance is a clue.

"I quit everything to become a musician. I made at least thirty bob a week—before tax. As things got worse, my parents could see less

David during the shooting of the film "Stardust"

sense in it—up and down the country and home ill, all for about 2p. They advised against it, but never ordered—and I never considered giving it up.

"I'm in a privileged position, now. That's what I got out of the East End for. I can decide for myself. One day I will wake up and decide it's time for a change—whatever feels right.

"I always found the 'art world' expressive, and I like being in it. I think my music shocked—it wasn't like David Cassidy, as some might have suspected. You either liked it or loathed it.

"So far, I have accumulated about five real friends and thousands of acquaintances in this business—but then, being an only child has made me rather insular. I suppose if I wasn't doing what I am, I'd be a farmer or something, because I have a tendency toward remote places. The country. I'm a semi-recluse, already.

"I have no image of myself in my own mind—that would be a mistake. I like what I'm doing, or I wouldn't be doing it. I must feel it—there can be no compromise. When the time comes and I have nothing else to offer, I will have gone already. I won't be a fallen idol.

David Essex is not responsible for his physical appearance. The fact that the pieces fell together with youthful precision is just another good luck charm. What he did do was to stretch himself and break out of the passive state. Develop his talents and push hard.

While we dream of his image and his lifestyle, it's best to remember—he worked hard for it— yet he's still just one of the boys. He still gives his wife Maureen a peck as he leaves for work (it might be a month in America!), he still sees his little girl Verity safely off to bed, and he still has to clean it up if Scruffy, the dog, makes a mess. Though somehow, he's still bigger than life.

"Every time I see my mum, she says I'm losing weight. She keeps a room at home, decorated with pictures of me all over the walls—but only the ones where I'm smiling. When I'm serious, she thinks I'm ill."

We should be so ill!

Leo Sayer

By Caroline Boucher

GERARD Sayer was born in Shoreham, a beautiful and quietly wealthy piece of the Sussex coast line, populated mainly by retired colonials. Apart from a few furtive dabbles into the music business in his late teens, when he lived in London's Notting Hill, young Sayer has always stuck to his beloved South coast, which has strongly influenced his song-writing.

Leo, as he is now called, is no newcomer to the music business. He was in groups—singing and playing mouth harp, since school, and has even sat in with Alexis Korner on occasions. He achieved no prominence, however, until he met up with Dave Courtney and Adam Faith. And even now he's successful, he has an immense distrust of the music business,

Leo Sayer: "I'm like the clown—happy on the outside and sad on the inside."

for the indifference it doled out to him in the early days.

"I remember doing gigs down at the Speakeasy, and other terrible gigs to indifferent audiences," says Leo. "I used to get so cheesed off I'd break into an impromptu blues—true blues, in the true sense of the word—and just tell the audience how rotten they were.

"Even when I came to audition my own band, I suddenly realised what a terrible standard of musicianship there is in Britain. I don't think I'd fully realised what audiences have to put up with until then.

"These people were coming in, asking to play full time in a band, and they couldn't play their instruments properly—disgraceful. I think everybody should be capable of being all-round entertainers."

Leo tends to think like a true blues singer. He can only sing songs he really believes in, and can identify with. In the old days when he sang with little bands, he found it virtually impossible to stand up onstage and sing banal lyrics.

"I have to write personal songs, I can't write any other sort. I've written about everything that has happened to me to date. I know they may come over as unhappy songs, but I was very happy as a child.

"I think everybody's the same—you tend to remember the upsets rather than the good times. I think people who notice only the good times are kidding themselves. You have to learn by your mistakes, and if you tend to look at all the great things you've done, you tend to grow up as an egomaniac."

The turning point in Leo's story came when, through Dave Courtney, he met Adam Faith. Adam became Leo's manager, guide and mentor, and Dave became his co-writer.

Dave—once drummer in Adam Faith's old backing band, the Roulettes—was holding auditions in Brighton to suss out the local talent, and along came Leo fronting a band called Patches.

Leo's extraordinary voice arrested him. He got a demo and took it round to Adam—it was very basic, just Leo singing to a piano—and Adam was equally struck. At the time he was in the middle of making the "Budgie" TV series, and too busy to do anything, but as soon as he left the series, in May 1972, he started to move.

Adam Faith with Leo Sayer.

Keith Altham, publicist for the Who, and long time friend of Adam's recalls: "Adam came up to the office at around that time with a cassette player, with Leo on it. I think it was the song—'Living In America'—that Warner Brothers subsequently put out as a single for Patches.

"I was immediately struck by the voice. He asked me to see the band down in Brighton, so I went down to some little gig in a pub. I wasn't particularly impressed by the band, but as soon as the kid got up to sing, his

voice was so incredible it bowled you over."

Keith played an important part in the Leo history, as he introduced Adam and Leo to Roger Daltrey. This came about because they wanted to record—preferably out of London, and somewhere inexpensive. Keith suggested the new studio Roger Daltrey had just finished building in his stables.

"I knew Adam and Roger would get on because they both had the same sort of background in London

Picture by Terry O'Neill

Brothers America heard of Leo and rushed people over in a frenzy to sign him up for USA rights, they had no idea he had once been signed to their UK label, and his contract let drop. They consequently paid about three times the amount for him.

"Silverbird" was recorded. It was an expensive album to make (£ 16,000), but Adam realised how vital it was for this first album and single to be good. From the material on it, he dreamed up the clown image, and the whole thing was launched simultaneously last September. Out came the album, accompanying stickers and posters, and the odd TV appearance, all depicting this extraordinary little person looking like a saddened monkey, got up in a clown suit. It certainly stuck in the memory, which is what it was supposed to do.

"I can hide behind the clown's outfit, which is nice to start out with," said Leo. "I'm a schizophrenic really, like the clown—happy on the outside and sad on the inside. I'm quite a happy person really, but whenever I turn my mind to music, or once I go onstage, I go into a whole emotional trip. I'm a blues singer really, and my whole life comes out in just that hour onstage."

At this point, Adam was positively masterful as a manager. He didn't allow Leo to become over exposed. The photos that were released of him were the very best, mainly by Terry O'Neill. The TV appearances were prestige ones, the interviews not over plentiful, and the gigs the same. Everyone's appetite was whetted but not satiated. Clever.

Leo did the Roxy Music tour of Britain and Europe at that time, and went down well. His backing band, including the excellent Jimmy Litherland of Mogul Thrash, was the best. The whole place was abuzz with him. And it all went as Adam had planned. He had been determined that Leo should be a star without having to travel up and down the MI in the back of a van, and that's how it was.

After that tour, Leo was off to America for the early part of 1974. Then back to do the next album and single.

Adam is unshakeably confident that Leo will shape musical history. He's probably right. He is also convinced he will be a millionaire. He's very probably right there too.

when they were young, and they've got the same sort of humour."

They got on like a house on fire. Roger lives only about twenty miles from Brighton (where Adam's businesses are based), and besides recording Leo, work started on Roger's solo album for which Leo and Dave Courtney co-wrote all the songs.

Leo couldn't have had a better introduction to the big time. Roger's solo album was a success, and drew a lot of attention. Every interview Roger did, he praised Leo and Dave to the skies. He was generous to a fault, and Leo's name began to stick here and there.

At the time Leo was signed to Warner Brothers with Patches. Track Records showed a brief interest in signing him through the Who connection, but nothing ever happened. The Patches single for Warner Brothers never did anything. despite being quite catchy. The group were not re-signed, and Chrysalis took them up. The story has it that when Warner

Elton John

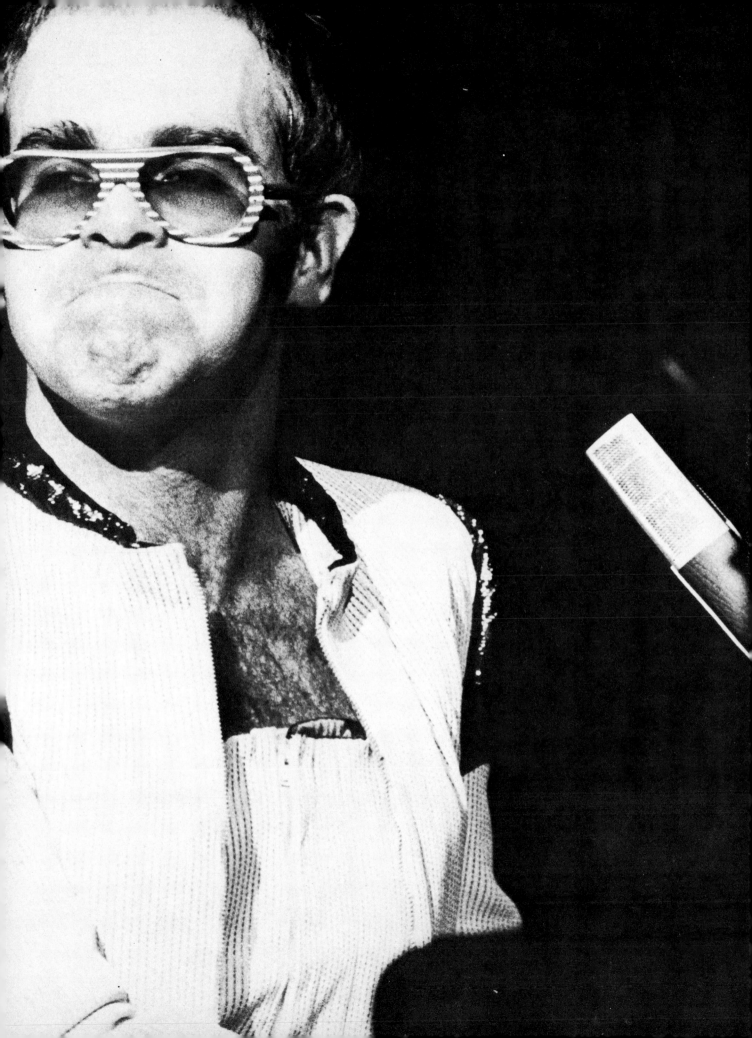

By Fox-Cumming

AS A RESULT of a hugely successful US tour, Elton John graduated in 1973 from being a dollar millionaire into a sterling one. The money doesn't matter, he says, since it wasn't for that that he came into the music business, but it is still some indication of his popularity.

While more outrageous artists hog the headlines in the process of making a quick kill, people forget that Elton is the number one British artist in America, enjoying sales figures second only to Stevie Wonder—and in his own country he's scarcely a prophet wothout honour.

In these times when a lithe figure and a photogenic face count almost as much as the music, Elton would be the first to admit that he hasn't made his name as a sex symbol.

"I'm not your rangy pin-up idol who looks good in a tight-fitting pair of jeans. That's partly why I wear outrageous clothes, and also there's a comedian streak somewhere in my personality."

That flair for the ridiculous was probably what started him out collecting glasses. He now has over 40 pairs of them, which travel with him in specially designed cases.

A lot of his glasses cost a fortune, but originally he didn't need to wear them at all. "I only put them on because I wanted to look like Buddy Holly."

But eventually they did become necessary, and by that time he'd dearly have liked to be rid of them. "But, as I couldn't get on with contact lenses, I was stuck with glasses, so I decided I might as well have some fairly flash ones." These include a pair fitted with windscreen wipers and another that have his name across the top in lights.

Elton's not only a collector of glasses. His home houses a vast collection of soft toys, and so many theatrical prints that there's no longer any room for them indoors. New additions to his collection have to be housed outside, in the garage.

Elton spends his wealth lavishly. He's a compulsive present buyer, never forgetting any birthday or anniversary. In fact bad memory and absent-mindedness is something he finds hard to tolerate in others.

But in work he is scarcely systematic. He tends to leave everything till the last minute, and the results are all the better for his doing so.

"When we come to make an album, Bernie Taupin scarcely ever has the lyrics ready more than about a week before we're due to start recording, and I'm still working on the music while the recording is going on.

"When we did 'Goodbye Yellow Brick Road' I wrote the music for the whole double album in four days flat. I'd get up at the crack of dawn and work to have something ready when the rest of the band got up and were ready to play."

Bernie and Elton got together in rather a strange way. Elton was playing with different bands and at the

Elton's word-man Bernie Taupin

same time writing tunes, but couldn't put any lyrics to them. Bernie had the opposite problem and eventually decided to do something about it by advertising for a tunesmith in the music press. Elton replied to the ad. and that's where it all began.

"We seldom worked together," recalls Elton. "Bernie would write his lyrics up in his Lincolnshire retreat and send them down to me: then I'd put music to them. Often he didn't hear the results until the records were out.

"He'd pop into the studios every now and again, but there was not really anything for him to do there and he'd be terribly bored if he had to stay all the time we were recording."

Now though, Bernie's moved down south to become Elton's near neighbour in Surrey, so they are be-ginning to work more closely together.

Obviously when a performer has been around as long as Elton has, the question crops up: "When are you going to give it all up."

The answer's simple: "Sometimes I get fed up with it all and feel like chucking it in for good, but when it came down to it I know I never could."

Should he ever get fed up, there are always his outside interests to sustain him. Despite his unathletic build, he's no mean sportsman. He plays an excellent game of tennis, swims well and plays a passable game of football. He uses soccer training as a means for keeping his weight down but his interest extends further than that. He's an avid fan of the game and a keen supporter of Watford Football Club. He's involved with the club's management and earlier this year played a benefit concert at their ground which raised several thousand pounds.

He's also done good work for the Invalid Children's Association, of which an old friend and admirer of his work, Princess Margaret, is president.

Another interest is The National Youth Theatre. He's on their board and gets down to watch rehearsals as often as he can. "They pull my leg unmercifully. It's nice for me to go somewhere where I'm not treated as a star, just an ordinary bloke."

Perhaps it was watching others acting that prompted Elton to have a go himself. The Pinball Wizard in "Tommy" was his first role, no doubt there will be others. It's not his fault that he hasn't been seen in acting roles more often.

"The trouble is that when people approach you to do something they tell you so-and-so and so-and-so will also be doing it and you think 'great'. Then you ring up the people involved and they don't know anything about it, or have changed their minds."

Some erudite reporter from a national paper recently had a listen to some of Elton's sadder songs and dubbed him a manic depressive. Nothing could be further from the truth. Once he's offstage that goonish humour takes over and he's a ball of energy, thinking what to do next.

"If music was my one and only interest," he says, "I'd go mad. You have to have some kind of outlet. Musicians who talk about nothing but music are so boring." Hear, Hear.

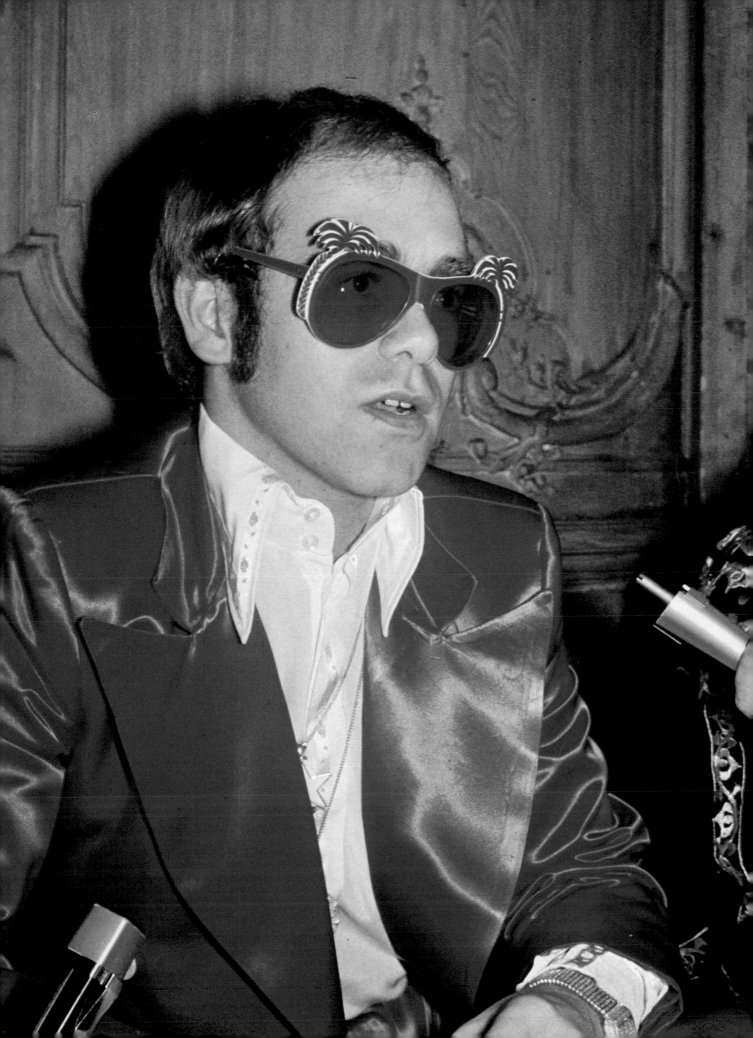

Gary Glitter

By Rosalind Russell

IF YOU EVER get backstage at a Gary Glitter concert, whatever you do, don't whistle in the dressing room. If you do let fly with a couple of carefree bars, you might find that the whole show will not only be called off, he might never speak to you again.

For Gary Glitter is a very superstitious man, and to a showman, the very worst thing you can do is cast a bad spell on the act. It's an old showbiz tradition that if someone whistles in the dressing room, it's a bad omen and the show will die a death.

"This stems back from when I was about 15 years old and I was doing a tour with a variety show on the Empire circuit. At that time, you played a town for a whole week, but if the first night didn't go well, the whole week's work was called off.

"On that same show there was Gerry Dorsey—now Engelbert Humperdink—and Vince Taylor and the Playboys (I don't know what happened to them). Anyway, I was right at the bottom of a bill of about 15 acts.

"I forgot about the warning and began to whistle in the dressing room on the first night of a week's show. There was this dancer in the room—he was very camp—anyway he flew at me saying 'the show will do badly, it'll be taken off and we'll all be out of work'. Well, it did. I felt everyone was looking daggers at me because it was my fault. I felt quite ostracised."

So ever since then, he's taken omens very much to heart and if things didn't bode well he'd be inclined to call a show off. He's also an avid reader of horoscopes.

"I read them everyday, even though I know it's a load of rubbish. I wouldn't miss them. I'm a Taurus. I think I'm very typical of my sign—very stubborn, very down to earth and inclined to be a bit on the chubby side . . ."

He grins. Gary has an almost constant battle with his waistline. He just can't afford to look at things which are fattening because he puts on weight so easily—really annoying for him when he sees manager and co-writer Mike Leander putting away big dinners and never gaining an ounce.

It's surprising, too, when you consider the amount of energy he expends onstage. Even when he is talking to you, he's moving around, making expansive gestures with his arms and getting up to illustrate points. When we met, he was having a frugal lunch of a slice of boiled ham and an orange—and I ate half of that!

"My weight is still going up and down like a yo-yo. When I'm working, touring that is, I need a decent meal just for the energy. I always have a couple of glasses of wine before I go onstage, but I sweat so much up there, when I come off I'm gasping for a few glasses of lager, so it all goes back on again. If I even have a couple of chips I put pounds on.

"Mind you, I've never once had a

letter from anyone saying I was too fat, or saying they didn't love me because I was fat. I think I'm a cuddly type of person . . .''

I doubt if "cuddly" is the adjective that leaps immediately to mind when you watch his stage show. Glitter has one of the most suggestive acts I've seen in my life. It beats me how he manages to get the same adulation from his audiences as they would give to David Cassidy or Donny Osmond.

Whatever age Gary professes to be—I think he owns up to 30 now—even if it's the truth, he's a generation away from Donny. Yet the

girls still scream, go potty and are carried from the front of the stage in droves.

At a thrust of the hip, or a pout of the lip, another hundred or so have collapsed, crying, overcome with emotion. He gets away with the old trick of teasing them from the edge of the stage, or getting down on his knees while he sings "Lonely Boy".

Behind all the theatrics, is Glitter a lonely boy? It's unlikely he has the time to be lonely, but when he does have a few hours to spare, he likes to spend them by himself, fishing.

After he slipped a disc on a tour of

Scandinavia, his vanity wouldn't let him wear the necessary corset—he said we wouldn't be able to see the much-vaunted hairy chest through a surgical corset. I suggested some sequins to brighten it up, but that didn't meet with a lot of enthusiasm either.

The real Gary Glitter—the man behind the image—is still a little vain. He's a fairly quiet person, a little shy of strangers, but very eloquent. He is completely absorbed in his work; realistic enough to know that the incredible peak he has reached with his singing and stage act can't last forever, he's full of ideas for a different future.

After completing his first film, "Remember Me This Way"—you'll remember the hit single of the same title—which was mostly a documentary of his life, he decided his next film would require some acting. By that I mean more acting than he does ordinarily.

"I'm not comparing myself to Robert Redford or Paul Newman by any means, but if you go and see them in a film, they are still themselves. They might grow a beard, or look a bit different, but they are still basically themselves in every movie. That's what the public pay to go and see. I believe my public will pay to go and see Gary Glitter, even though I play a role within that.

"In 'Remember Me This Way', there was only one real bit of acting. That came when I was supposed to be talking to this chick on the phone—which was difficult because of course there was no one on the other end of the phone.

"These three guys come in and I have to do a bit of Kung Fu on them. I have to smash one bloke's head through a balsa wood table. Well I did it, and he didn't get up again. I'd knocked him unconscious! If that had been me, I wouldn't have come round for a week."

Gary went through all the Kung Fu actions, alarming me because he has a bad back and I expected him to lock in a painful position at any minute.

His own taste in films is fairly wide. He enthused wildly about Robert Redford in The Sting, but doesn't go too much on violent films. He enjoys the old Dracula movies—as long as he doesn't have to sit and watch them on his own.

"I suppose I'm a bit of a grasshopper really," he says. OK Kung Fu!

arpenters

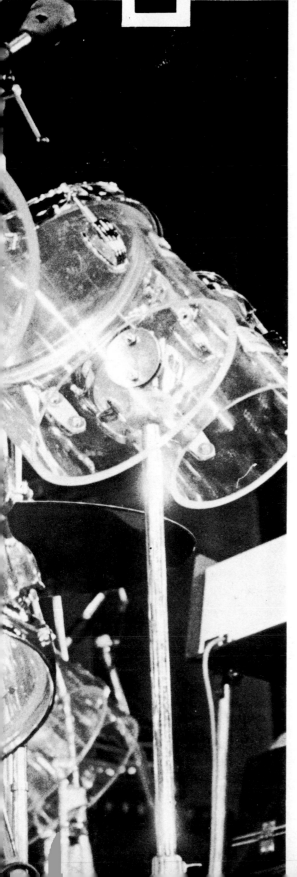

By Beverley Legge

IT'S NOT easy being a Carpenters fan. In fact you have to work at it. Don't let me discourage you, but there are all sorts of reasons for you giving up before you ever start.

You see the trouble really lies with the Carpenters themselves. It's their image. Despite their enormous record sales, the duo have never really fitted in with the contemporary music scene.

No doubt there are aspects of their act which tie in with current trends, but taken as a whole the band stand out as being quite out of place amongst today's hitmakers.

Of course any attempt to put Rich-

54

ard and Karen into the rock category is instantly doomed to failure. Their albums and singles often outsell many of today's leading rock outfits. Even so what the Californian duo have to offer is sadly unacceptable to the majority of hard-core rock addicts.

One or two braver rock enthusiasts may in an unguarded moment buy a Carpenters record, but they do so only with a feeling of great uneasiness. The truth is it isn't too hip to dig the brother and sister team.

Their clean-cut image and their general unhysterical approach to music have disqualified them from a place amonst the royal family of rock.

Other musicians might be upset by this state of affairs, but Richard remains unperturbed. Neither he nor Karen have any desire to be taken for something they're not.

"I suppose when we first entered the business people made the mistake of putting us in as part of the rock scene. They seemed to think that we were rock music and that we thought we were rock music. But we're not. We're not even soft rock. We're really pop, which is a whole different scene."

All of which only goes to prove the point that finding the right category to place the outfit in is not an easy task. Even fans of the duo are confused.

Pop stars' images tend to be somewhat outlandish and amazingly notorious, but when it comes to Richard and Karen quite the reverse is true. In a world peopled by long-haired, scandal ridden stars, both stand out as being disconcertingly clean-cut and well-scrubbed.

It's not an image which draws the headlines, but it can certainly attract comments from the cynics. Richard knows them off by heart.

"We've been called stickly-sweet' goody two shoes and squeaky clean, and a whole lot of other things, by music critics. To me a music critic should be concerned with music rather than dress or cleanliness.

"When we came out in 1969 it was right in the middle of the acid rock period, when all performers suffered from this, 'take me as I am' attitude. We arrived on the scene, just as normally clean people, and naturally we stood out."

"I'm not too concerned about our image. I just feel that it has got a little

too far over to one side. In other words we've been made out to be just a little too clean. Like nobody could be that clean.''

Even so their image still remains one of the most clean-cut and conventional of today's pop acts, and unlike a lot of their competitors in the chart their thoughts on politics and current affairs are totally moderate.

For instance, ask Karen her opinion on the rights of women and you'll get an answer something like this: ''some people seem to think I'm something of a Women's Lib symbol, because I'm a girl drummer. But to be quite honest, I've never really got into Women's Lib.

''I've achieved success in my profession and I lead a strenuous life but none of this takes away from my being a woman. I think it's up to every woman to live her life the way she wants to. Not the way some political movement would have her lead it.''

So much for Karen. What about Richard? This time on the subject of pollution. ''If you halted all cars, planes and refineries and industries just because they're polluting the air, where would you be?

''It would be ideal if we could preserve our environment and continue to make technological progress, but until someone discovers how, we'll have to wrestle with some necessary compromises.'' Not exactly what you might call extremism.

Perhaps the one song of theirs, which dosen't fit in with this clean-cut, moderate image is ''Superstar''. On first hearing it seems to be a fairly innocuous song on the theme of unrequited love, but on closer inspection it proves to be a groupie's lament.

''No, the lyrics don't fit in with our image, but they didn't really seem to offend anyone,'' explains Richard. ''We only had to change one word in the whole song.

''Nowadays you could do it, but at that time Top 40 radio in America would not have played something that said, 'can hardly wait to sleep with you again.' So I changed it to 'be with you again.'

''We got some letters asking us what it was about, so perhaps a lot of the kids didn't understand. But we didn't get many complaints. The one that got lots of letters against it was 'Goodbye To Love'. People didn't like the guitar solo at the end. To a lot of

our fans that was like hard rock and they wrote in to complain about us changing our style.''

Broadly speaking 'middle of the road' is the term most applicable to the Carpenters' sound. But there are still small details about the band that don't quite fit in with that description.

For instance that fuzz guitar solo that Richard spoke about in 'Goodbye To Love', or the lyrics of 'Superstar'. And what about the fact that Karen is a drummer. There can't be many m-o-r bands that sport a female percussionist.

Just in case any one has any ideas that a girl drummer in a m-o-r band is a joke, Karen has some knowing words on the subject: ''People always think a girl playing drums is some kind of a gimmick, but that isn't the case with me. I take my playing very seriously. I'm a great fan of people like Joe Morello and Buddy Rich.''

But drumming is only a minor issue when considering the success of the twosome. The real selling point of every Carpenter record must surely be Karen's incredible voice, followed closely by Richard's ability as an arranger and occasionally as a composer.

There is however one other point which has greatly assisted their climb to stardom, and strangely enough it's a point which is seldom written about.

It is Richard's uncanny ability to keep picking different types of songs and yet still achieve massive sales with each one. Songs like 'Close To You', 'Goodbye To Love', 'Yesterday Once More' or 'Jambayala' illustrate this only too well.

This is a deliberate policy on Richard's part to vary their releases as much as possible.

''I think a lot of groups make a mistake by following up a very successful record with a similar one. We've never wanted to do that. One of the things that impressed me about the Beatles was that they never brought out two similar records in succession. I think that was one of the keys to their success.''

And certainly one of the keys to the Carpenters success.

Roxy

Early Roxy at Crystal Palace.

Roxy's Andy Mackay

Bryan Ferry

By Fox-Cumming

YOU WOULD think that anyone who against all the odds had managed to launch a successful band in just a few months, would be over the moon or at least a bit arrogant about it. But not Bryan Ferry.

The front man of that jauntily named band Roxy Music is neither jolly nor big-headed. The only positive emotion he displays to any marked degree is an excessive sensitiveness to criticism. He visibly smarts at some of the things that have been said about him.

"I do enjoy performing, I do love recording," he says without showing a spark of life about either.

It's impossible to know whether Ferry's acting out a part or whether he's just naturally evolved into his present public persona. At any rate, the guy who started out looking like a rather spry young accountant has somehow managed to become more equated with decadence than anyone else on the British rock scene.

The lank dyed-black hair and the increasingly pallid complexion, both beautifully photographed in 'Death In Venice'-like poses have obviously helped, but the change has gone further than that. The near-benevolent sneer that used to contort his face in the early days when he stood at the piano in archetypal rocker fashion has given way to a totally unsmiling visage above a white tuxedo. He apes the 30's crooners to a 'T' but somehow there's no conscious effort to please. He comes over like a tired actor at the end of a long run, but manages at the same time to remain very watchable.

"Decadence," he questions with a languid flick of his wrist, "what is decadence? I don't know." Maybe he doesn't live with 15 Chinese girls and boys of assorted ages, maybe he doesn't live in a crumbling castle with walls covered in colourless moss, but decadent he still seems.

In interviews he tends to sit, head slumped on chest, mumbling out answers so quietly that you have to strain to catch what he's saying. The liveliest things about him are the snorts that punctuate his sentences. Perhaps he has sinus trouble?

Often, particularly in the American Rock Press, Bryan's name is linked with Bowie's, but they are as different as chalk and cheese. Bowie's obsession with the future is completely at odds with Ferry's fascination for the past.

If Lou Reed, with his tales of seamier-side Sixties, is considered out of date, then Bryan with his borrowings from the Thirties and earlier, must be nearly as dead as a dodo, but he's not.

In conversation he may come over as infuriatingly vague and inaudible, but onstage, for all the lack of energy, he does have presence. That curious voice, unmatchable with any character you've ever come across, is strangely compelling.

In the early days when it was delivering "Virginia Plain" it could possibly have been taken as humourous. Now there's no doubt. Even with the obvious pastiche of Dylan's "A Hard Rain's Gonna Fall", it's deadly earnest. Mr. Ferry is not there to have fun poked at him. Somehow he gets away with it.

It's no good accusing him of running Roxy like a dictator. He'll only answer that he wishes he'd never called the band Roxy Music in the first place and named it after himself instead. After all, the band is his concept, he is the principal ideas man. By and large the others just provide the musical expertise to bring his ideas to fruition.

You can't accuse him of cowardice either. After being given a terrible pasting in the Press for his first solo album, about which admittedly most people later had second thoughts, he was quite unworried about going ahead with a second in similar mould. Let the set-'em-up and knock-'em-down merchants have as much say as they like, Bryan Ferry won't lie down and obligingly die for them.

When Roxy Music first appeared onstage looking very Fifties, many people thought that they would soon become hidebound by their own concept. But at the time Bryan remained unruffled. "I don't find the concept in the least constricting. There's plenty of room to adapt it as we go along."

Adapt it he did. By the time the band were performing material from their third album onstage, the Fifties look had almost gone. Bryan was no longer anchored in a black cat suit to his keyboards, but centre stage and dressed immaculately in evening dress, crooning against a background of palm fronds and elegant ruins.

Occasionally he'd still do a quick palais glide over to the keyboards for the odd quick trill, but seemed basically content to play the ultra smooth lounge lizard.

He's no great mover, but then he doesn't need to be. His stage character is more than satisfactorily put across with just the occasional tired mannerism and the odd list of shoulders from port to starboard and back.

The indolent image that Bryan portrays onstage does not spill over into his working life.

Somehow without ever seeming to move much faster than snail's pace he gets his solo ventures done, writes and records enough material to keep his band busy and still manages to put in enough live appearances to keep his fans happy, in Britain on the Continent and in the States.

And there seems no reason to suppose that he won't be able to carry on doing just that until he's old and grey as a badger.

Eno

By Fox-Cumming

"POOR old Eno," they all said when that gentleman was carted off to hospital with a collapsed lung early in 1974. Not just because a collapsed lung is not a particularly nice thing to have, but because it had meant cancelling half of his British tour with the Winkies, his first major outing as a solo performer.

But for Eno himself it was a blessing in disguise. He'd wanted to do some concerts sure enough, but somehow the tour had become much longer than he'd originally envisaged, and when he actually got up onstage, he found it much less of a buzz than he might have expected.

"I was totally detached. I found myself thinking about the next day's shopping while I was singing."

His illness, therefore, gave him a chance to mark time and think out his next moves. Once he'd convalesced, there was no move to reschedule the cancelled dates. Eno retreated to his Maida Vale home with his cats and his tapes and seemed all the happier for it.

He makes no claims to be a musician as such. He plays no single instrument with any marked degree of proficiency. He's just an eccentric boffin who's never more content than when he's experimenting with different sounds and ways of projecting them in his workshop, using synthesisers, his now famous electric larynx or any other gadget he's either found or invented.

His own album "Here Come The Warm Jets" was a good one, and fairly successful commercially. Had his sudden illness not prevented him from giving it full promotion, it would have been a monster. But it's his work with other people that seems to give him the most satisfaction.

The "No Pussyfooting" album he made with Robert Fripp opened up possibilities for him that he's still keen to carry on exploring.

He's also batted a few ideas around with individual members of Roxy Music and more lately begun work with John Cale, one of his heroes. Eno's long idolised the work of the old Velvet Underground and on that ill-fated tour paid tribute to them by including one of their numbers, *"What Goes On."*

At his home, he has rack after rack

full of tapes—miles and miles of recorded experiments that may or may not get used. "Nothing ever gets thrown away," he says.

"Sometimes tapes may sit up there for years before I take them down and give them another listen, to see if there's anything I can use. Sometimes things that were mistakes at the time turn out to be very interesting."

Part of his fascination with The Portsmouth Sinfonia, the orchestra that can't play, is that the mistakes made by the players are always undeliberate but to him an endless source of new ideas.

Despite the weirdness of some of his output, he makes no bones about borrowing ideas from other people. "I'm a natural born thief.

"Since I'm no great guitarist, when I'm working with guitar I have to use what few sequences I know. It's not at all restricting though. For example," he says, playing a chord sequence that sounds instantly familiar, "dozens of hit songs have been written around that sequence. And," he adds with a smile, "by the time I've finished there'll be a lot more!"

One of Eno's interests is film scores. He did one for a little-known avant-garde movie.

"It was a film of images on loops superimposed so that they provided a kind of collage without you ever seeing exactly the same thing twice. I decide to fit the music to the pictures exactly by putting a series of sounds on loops to coincide with the film spools. I think it worked very well and I'd like to do more of that kind of thing."

A lot of Eno's musical ideas are based on simple repetition. He'll put a sound on a loop so that it occurs at regular intervals and build up from there, using either more loops or instruments making 'one-off' sounds.

It's doubtful if in the future Eno will want to embark on tours as such again. He's much more likely to make the odd concert appearance with friends he happens to be working with at the time.

In between times he'll be found in his laboratory turning out his weird and wonderful sounds until the day the synthesiser can compute for itself and make him redundant.

"But that," he says, eyeing it suspiciously, "will never happen. I can always pull its plug out."

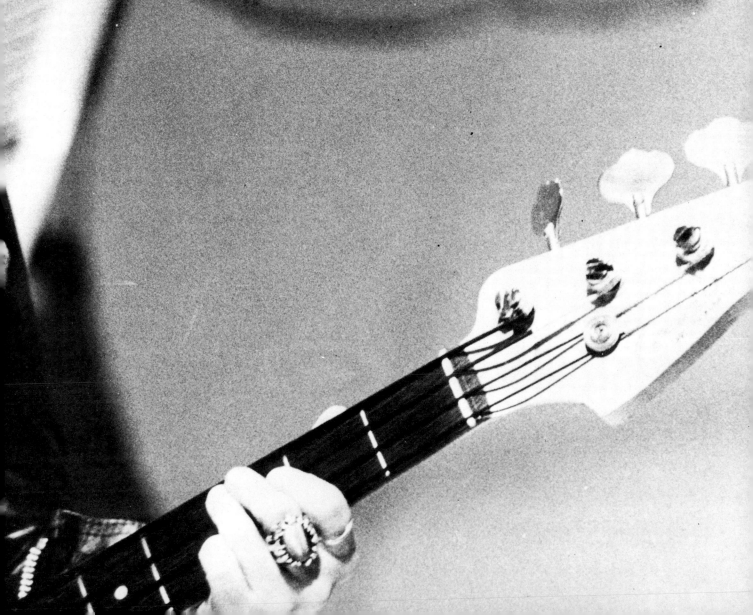

Suzi Quatro

WHEN Suzi Quatro blistered our ears with her first hit single, "Can The Can", in 1973, her arrival took the whole music business by storm, even though we'd come to expect a female counterpart to Sweet, Gary Glitter, Bolan, and so on.

Suzi, clad in leathers and as verbally punchy as any hardened rock star, fitted the role perfectly.

Record producing millionaire Micky Most found her in Detroit, while on a trip to the States to work with Jeff Beck. He saw her raw potential, brought her back to England and made her a star.

"The only effect the music business has had on me is that I swear too much and drink more than's good for me. But as for the material things which success inevitably brings—well they don't really interest me. Money won't change the basic Suzi Quatro because I'm a bit too wise for that. All I want in life is to be able to write and play music—even if it's only for myself.

"I first started playing when I was eight. My father had a jazz band which needed a bongo player, and I happened to fill the vacancy. Then at 14 I joined my sisters in a band called Suzi Soul and the Pleasure Seekers. They all had nice legs and bosoms, so I had to make up for my lack of those by making as much noise as I could.

"We must have been mad to have gone out on gigs with a name like that, but we were so young we didn't understand the connections people might put to the group's name. Looking back it was great fun. We used to support the real big names sometimes, including Mitch Rider and the Detroit Wheels and the MC5."

Within a year of "Can The Can" Suzi had chart successes with 48 Crash, Daytona Demon, Devil Gate Drive and Satin Silk, all from the most successful songwriter/producer combination in the country—Nicky Chinn and Mike Chapman.

On one occassion I joined Suzi in the studio to watch her record a single—48 Crash. While Chinn and Chapman lay down the law, Suzi in her wild way reacts with an odd kind of discipline, obeying them to the point of injecting all her own feelings into a record.

"I prefer playing gigs to recording and to begin with, I found it hard to adjust to a studio. It usually takes me a while to warm up, but once I've got the same feelings towards a studio session as to a live gig, then I can really get down to working."

Suzi's band, drawn from all walks of the music business, have developed into a fine backing trio. Lead guitarist Len Tuckey is Suzi's mentor, and just for the record—her guardian as well. Pianist Alistair McKenzie and drummer Dave Neal join forces to hammer out the basic beat of repetitive riffs which are contained on all Quatro records.

"I like to look upon myself as just one of the band, although I'm always the boss. People always seem to think that because I'm a woman I can't do things as good as a man—well that's rubbish. Often I'm better."

But for all Suzi Q's hardness, deep down there's a real lady. She just has to be like she is to stop people trampling her into the ground.

"Sure I'm a woman—but I like to keep my womanly charms for the bedroom," she once told me over a game of snooker, another of her masculine pastimes.

Suzi's mind is one that gives the impression that she just thinks about being an exhibitionist. But once you get to know her really well, then you discover that she cares about people and about life.

In her tiny flat, she finds Sundays the biggest drag. But in her solitude, she finds the time to think about all the things that have happened to her. And Suzi's mental reactions and statements referring to them are incredibly penetrating.

"You know, performing is a very important part of me. I always try and kick the bad out of people, by trying to make them think about the things I say to them. Ever since I can remember, I've had this feeling that I'm gonna die really early, so I've started to write a whole work of really personal poems.

"Nobody has ever seen them and no one is gonna until I'm dead. I get the feeling that I've lived on Earth before, and that the Suzi Quatro of today is really a reincarnation of somebody who lived hundreds of years ago," confided Q.

While hit records are usually the passport to instant success, Quatro just sees them as a conveyor of what her music is really about. She's never written a single, leaving that commercial chore to Chinn and Chapman.

"I really wish I'd written Devil Gate Drive, but I just can't write things that are short. I guess being a lady means that I talk too much, and therefore I can't get all I wanna say into a three minute song.

"I write most of my songs with Len. But most of our material is only suitable for albums. Our first one was a real gas of an album, but the second one is gonna be the best thing you've ever heard."

Being a female in a predominatly male world has presented Suzi with a lot of hassles. Her early gigs found guys whistling and making improper suggestions to her.

"Now that I've made it, people don't like it. I'm a great one for getting ripped-off, but I don't care, because they know that deep down they can't take anything away from me.

"Suzi Quatro's made it on her own, and I intend to carry on doing just that. It's one thing to make the big time, but it's another thing to be able to sustain it. But I know that I have the talent to do it, so I'm not bothered what people might say about me."

At only 23, Suzi Q's made her mark on the British music scene. In just one year she conquered most of the barriers which force many female artists into liquidation.

For an artist to play a guitar that's bigger than herself, Suzi's a pretty small animal. But her style and talent are enormous. To begin with it appeared to be rather like the story of David and Goliath, with Goliath being the music biz and the general public . . . And look who won.

Little Miss Quatro's here for a long time to come, make no mistake about that.

By Mike Benton

(Above) Paul and Linda McCartney

(Right) Rod Stewart with Ron Wood

David Cassidy

THAT David Cassidy became an actor is not a surprise. His parents, Jack Cassidy and Evelyn Ward, are both actors. And that David Cassidy became a star is almost no surprise.

Actors in television series have a habit of becoming stars, and combining David's weekly tv performances with the excitement he created as a recording artist, there was no place for David to go but the top.

Yet it is incredible that it took such a short span in years for David to skyrocket from a young unknown to an international celebrity.

Certainly it required more than being born into an acting family, living in Hollywood, and being an appealingly handsome young man. Whatever it took, David had it and in his role as Keith Partridge in the television series *The Partridge Family*, he became well-known to viewers in over 30 countries around the world.

His concert tours through England, Holland, Germany, and France were complete sell-outs and frenzied illustration that his popularity was not "confined" to television.

Concerts in New Zealand, Australia and Japan provided David with more public assurances of devotion and adulation, and it was necessary to add extra appearances to his sched-

From Jean Lewis Hollywood Editor 16 Magazine

ule to accommodate the ticket demand.

By the age of 24, David had earned eight gold records, performed to a capacity audience in New York City's Madison Square Garden—an impressive record for any performer. Even one twice his age.

It all began in New York City on April 12, 1950, when David was born to singer-actor Jack Cassidy and Evelyn Ward. His mother was also an actress, and David remembers "wanting to be a performer since the first time I saw my father on the Broadway stage." David was three!

His parents were divorced when David was five, and he spent the next five years in West Orange, New Jersey, with his mother and grandparents. Then he and his mother moved to Hollywood, where he entered Emerson Junior High School and graduated from Rexford, a private school in Beverly Hills.

Following graduation, David spent

a year working with the Los Angeles Theatre Group and was featured in its production of And So To Bed.

His next move was back to New York City—where he lived with his father and stepmother Shirley Jones. He did summer stock and studied at the David Craig School of Musical Comedy.

During this time he won a co-starring role in the Broadway musical The Fig Leaves are Falling and subsequently got better reviews than the show. The show closed after three performances and David returned to Hollywood.

The next months were busy ones, and David was all over television, often beating out better established actors for roles, on virtually every major series on the air.

"It was incredible how it happened. I'd walk in, read, and immediately be sent to wardrobe. I kept thinking 'it's not supposed to be this easy!' but I was not about to argue with anybody," David smiles as he remembers his own reaction to those early casting calls.

Then, as they say, history was made. David tested for a new series The Partridge Family. His stepmother, Shirley Jones, had already been signed to play the mother, but until they'd settled on David, the

show's producers did not know they were related. And, when David auditioned, he didn't know that Shirley was going to be in the series.

The first single by the Partridge Family, *"I Think I Love You"*, featuring David on lead vocal, was released in August, 1970, just before the show's debut. It sold 5½ million copies, and is still selling! Seven albums followed, all certified Gold by the Record Industry Association of America, indicating sales of $1-million or more.

Meanwhile, David launched a parallel career as a solo recording artist, and his first single, *"Cherish"*, was also certified Gold. More singles followed, and albums, and each suggested a continuing growth as a recording artist, as David showed greater confidence and maturity.

Not content to "loaf" during his breaks from the television series, David's next move was to the concert stage and his first performance in April, 1971, at the Seattle (Wash.) Auditorium. He was described by Variety, show business trade paper, as "arriving with the force of an atomic bomb."

That concert debut was indicative of what was to come, and membership of the David Cassidy Fan Club zoomed beyond a phenomenal 200,000.

It became necessary to increase security during performances, and execute cloak-and-dagger getaways in fast cars. There was always the threat of physical danger to David, as well as to his fans, with their eagerness to be just-a-little-bit-closer.

It was just such demonstrations of love and devotion that caused David to treasure and zealousy guard his privacy.

He had to move several times as his Hollywood residence became too well known and hundreds of fans—who just wanted an extra glimpse—camped outside his door. Not only making it impossible for David to come and go quietly, but trampling his well-kept lawn and flowers.

Later David bought a ranch in Hawaii. And it began to attract him more and more frequently, for long stretches of time.

In a few short, relaxed responses, David explains why he goes there: "To think. To ride. To surf. To skindive. To relax."

Then his hazel eyes crinkle and get that special twinkle, and David confesses he spends long stretches of time "just watching the grass grow."

Considering that David Cassidy has become a substantial part of the landscape of the world, that's almost tantamount to confessing that he's watching himself grow.

An occupation he shares with the rest of us.

Marc Bolan

By Rosalind Russell

IT'S GROSS indecency. Here we are, through another summer, and Marc Bolan still hasn't fulfilled the prophecies of the critics who said he'd be long buried by now. What is it about the guy that keeps him hanging on?

It can't be just good looks, because many other artists, just as pretty, have dropped by the wayside—but Bolan seems to have something of the quality that Cliff Richard possesses.

He is adaptable enough to change to his musical surroundings. He also has an incredible ego that won't allow him to think of personal failure. Bolan is his own best publicity man.

"I'm incredibly flash," he admits with disarming honesty. It would be easy to put him down if he didn't own up to characteristics like this, but through it all, he still sees the entire situation as a joke.

He talks of ordering a pink Cadillac with leopard shin upholstery, fully aware that he won't ever be able to use it while he's working because it would get destroyed by over-eager fans, looking for souvenirs. That doesn't make it a practible proposition unless he uses it for running down to the shops for a can of beans now and again.

But Bolan doesn't even drive. He has Alfie, his friend and personal bodyguard to do that.

And if you've seen the size of Alfie, you'll know why no one ever tangles with him. He and Bolan are like brothers. In fact they seem closer than any of the others in the group. Mickey Finn spends his time with his own friends, and the rest don't even get as much limelight as he does.

"I'm happy to be doing what I'm doing," says Mickey. "I don't feel that I'm in the shadows and I don't want to be the centre of attraction."

When Alfie was involved in a car accident in 1974, he was quite badly hurt. Marc immediately saw to it that he had the best medical attention.

"It was good to be able to make sure he was sent to the best people. That's when it's good to have money," said Marc.

"I'm incredibly rich," he admits. "But I wouldn't say I was aware of money. I never carry any—not usually more than about ten bob. The only thing it has really bought me is a sense of freedom, in a crazy kind of way."

From an early age, Bolan has dreamt of being famous. If he hadn't done it this way, no doubt he would have found another, but it seems a remote dream when you belong to a family that is not rich and doesn't ever seem likely to be.

Bolan used to help his mother out on a fruit stall in the East End of London. His brother is a lorry driver, and now his father is caretaker of a block of flats. Bolan's grandma is a char lady. All of this is a very ordinary background to the life of a very public figure.

"The pop papers make you into a superstar—I don't believe in it at all," said the man who helped pave the way for so many other glitter merchants. "I can't walk onstage without having to be nine feet tall to live up to all the expectations.

"There's no way man. It puts tremendous demands on you. Just because you've got a Rolls Royce or something they think you're somebody else. It's pure nonsense."

Of course, he could always buy a mini and no one would notice at all, but it's only part of Bolan's contradictions. He makes them constantly, and generally the downbeat ones are when he's feeling a little over-exposed.

For a while, the papers were heavily down on the guy, seeing his end. When he made an effort and hit back by doing a sell-out tour, they billed it a "comeback".

"The press were all talking about this 'comeback' well I'd almost begun to believe it myself . . ." An all time low for Bolan, the man with the Divine Right complex.

But he got the nerve from some hidden resource and bopped right back, stronger than ever. "I'm not trying to prove anything, that's not my gig."

There can't be many artists who would dare to appear on Top of the Pops to do his record, completely without the backing band, and carry it off—but he did it.

You have to admire him for his brass neck, even if you don't like him. He has a tremendously friendly personality, and if you met him and still weren't won over, then I'd be really surprised. "I can be very Marc Bolan

though," he warns. "I can say 'have that person removed' and he is." A regal flick of the wrist, followed by a wicked grin. "Ultimately, I'm the most starish person I know dear."

But with his fans, he is very kind. There is a small clutch of girls standing on the opposite side of the road from the office we are in. Now and again he glances up, or gets up to fetch another Vodka and tonic. The girls all squeal and wave, and he waves back. A bit like making appearances from the Royal balcony at Buckingham Palace.

There is a constant little band of girls outside his London flat at Marble Arch, but it's only rarely he makes any real attempt to avoid them. Once or twice he has slipped out, dressed in scruffy old clothes so that no one will recognise him.

It'll be a sad day for rock and roll when a character like Boley can walk down the road unrecognised and unheralded. It's hard to see how long he can keep going in his present musical field and he ain't the type to go into cabaret like so many other artists past their prime. He has of course made the film Born To Boogie, with Ringo. And many other film plans have been mooted.

Bolan is so good at acting the part of Bolan, he'll have some difficulty losing the part to be anyone else. He's become typecast and it'll take a lot of effort to work at another character.

He doesn't make too many appearances—possibly because of his fear of overexposure again—and he hasn't attempted another public tour of the States. We can't know exactly what happened there, but the truth would appear to lie between the critics who were hoping he would die a death and reported the same, and Bolan's own claims of tremendous ovations.

But who needs America? "I know we're the biggest group in Britain," says Boley. "I can feel it in the air; I know it in the sales."

So how is he going to keep this up through the times we see very little of him? "Well my next thing won't have anything to do with glam rock. I'm not into second generation rock. I'm an innovator."

Paul McCart

By Rosie Horide

IT WAS the year of the Beatle rumours: Beatles to reform; Beatles to tour; Beatles to record again; in 1974 phases like that were bandied round the music business and the papers.

In many cases it was largely wishful thinking, but the fact that the group's legal wrangles were nearing their end added some substance to the stories.

Further fuel was added to the fire when it was reported that they were all speaking to each other again. Paul told me at the time: "There isn't any bitterness left between us now, so I suppose forming a band again is a possibility. But we're all rather too involved with our own things a the moment."

That didn't however stop them all lending a hand with Ringo's album: "All any of them had to do was ask," Paul said, "and Ringo did." So there were all the Beatles on one al-

bum—and that set off the rumours again with a vengeance.

Just about the only people who weren't caught up in these rumours were the Beatles themselves. Paul was all the time going about the business of re-forming his shattered Wings. Denny Seiwell and Henry McCulloch had left him just before the group went off to Lagos to record "Band On The Run", leaving Paul, Linda and the faithful Denny Laine to improvise.

"It wasn't easy, sounding like a whole group. But we all did a bit of everything, and it came out O.K., didn't it?" he asked.

That was something of an understatement. "Band on the Run" was generally acclaimed as one of the best ex-Beatle solo albums, and certainly the finest McCartney himself has made since the Beatles broke down irretrievably at the end of the '60s.

"Actually, I was pretty pleased with the final result, although nothing's ever perfect," was Paul's comment when I asked whether he really thought it was only O.K. "I think the album really captures the sound I want Wings to project."

But Paul couldn't possibly carry on Wings with just the three of them, so it was audition time again, and the re-building process began. The first replacement was easy to find. By a strange quirk of fate he and his predecessor had the same surname, McCullough.

This time, instead of Henry they got Jimmy. Since the unhappy demise of Stone the Crows, Jimmy had had a brief spell with that underrated band Blue, and now he was free again. Paul snapped him up.

The choice of drummer was a little more difficult. "I would have liked Ringo," said his ex-colleague, "but I understand he's busy at the moment!"

"The reason I got bored towards the end of the Beatles was because we hadn't performed to a live audience for years. Being on the road is what it's all about, seeing an audience out there and having the feeling that they're right there with you. So I want Wings to be a working band."

Breaking in a new band wasn't easy the first time, but then Paul had the formidable Beatles' legend to escape. Second time round it was bound to be a bit easier.

"By now I think many of the kids that are listening to our music don't even remember the Beatles. I'm sure some think Wings is the only band I've been in."

Maybe. But what's certain is that the old McCartney charisma is still there. And the screams he attracts merely by appearing on stage should be the envy of many younger artists. The fact that he's now over thirty doesn't seem to have worried the current pop fans, who scream at him just as they would Donny or David.

Paul himself has matured however. And much as he loves having a band, there are a lot of other things to occupy his time. He's already had great success with theme tunes—like his "Live and Let Die" soundtrack and the signature tune for TV's "Zoo Gang".

"Doing things like that is a great opportunity to get into another field: it's like films, something different. It's nice to be able to do that occasionally, although I might not want to get away from it all the time."

Also for a change, Paul has done some work on other people's records this year. He produced his brother Mike McGear's album at Strawberry Studios in Stockport—the ones which 10 CC always use. Paul and Linda also persuaded Scaffold (Mike's Group) to get back into the singles world with "Liverpool Lou".

"I really enjoyed doing those recordings, so I expect we'll do some more work together in the future."

With that, the Wings film which is still in the process of being finished (it's reportedly going to be called "The Bruce McMouse Show") and a re-vitalised Wings on the road, Paul hardly has any spare time.

But when he does there's always his house in London, the farm in Scotland, his wife and the three children Heather, Mary and Stella. And what about the famous Old English steepdog Martha? They alone would be enough to keep any ordinary man occupied.

But then Paul McCartney has never been ordinary, and it's pretty certain that in years to come we'll be looking back on a whole host of extra accomplishment of McCartney the man and musician.

Kiki Dee

WHEN Kiki Dee's *"Amoureuse"* became a hit, the mere mention of her name brought pleased smiles to the faces of everyone who knew her.

So many people had been wanting her to make it for so long, and as Elton John, to whose record label Rocket she is signed, says: "If anyone's paid their dues, it's Kiki. She richly deserves all the success she can get."

Before she signed to Rocket, Kiki's career was a story of wrong directions and false starts. She began, at the age of 16, as a cabaret-ish singer, and later came to London and signed to Philips. Her time with them was not marked by any spectacular successes, and eventually they parted company.

Then came what appeared to be the chance of a lifetime. She was asked to go to America as the first-ever white girl signing to Motown. But when she got there she found Motown in a state of upheaval, shifting offices and changing policies. After about 18 months she'd made a few records, but again nothing had happened to make her career take off.

So a disappointed Kiki returned to Britain and the cabaret circuit, until Elton John contacted her and signed her up to Rocket.

"More than anything else," says Kiki, "Elton gave me back my confidence. After all that had gone before, I was feeling very unsure of myself."

"She was frightened of her own shadow," according to Elton. "Wouldn't have had the nerve to say boo to a goose."

By Fox-Cumming

Before she joined Rocket, Kiki had never written any songs that anyone had ever heard. "I'd tinkered around with a couple of things, but I was too nervous to play them to anyone."

Elton encouraged her to write and in the end four of her own compositions appeared on her album "Loving And Free", and they were well-enough received for Kiki to begin to think of herself as a budding singer songwriter.

After "Amoureuse" broke, Kiki got a band together, and after a few minor teething troubles and early line-up changes they went out on the road. Immediately they faced the problem of wanting to play uptempo funky material to audiences that expected a set full of "Amoureuses", and the hit single began to seem a mixed blessing.

"It's a great song and I love singing it," said Kiki at the time, "but it's not really representative of what we want to do, and I don't want to get into the position of having to put out a string of material in that vein. It would only be misleading."

Gradually audiences began to know what to expect of the band. Kiki who'd always been rather a restrained performer, began to open up. "I've always felt that when I'm getting near to really getting across, I always seem to hold back, but it's getting easier all the time."

"We're taking things very slowly. After all, this band was put together. It's not made up of people who've been friends for years, so we need time to really get to know each other.

"I don't want to be considered as a solo singer with a backing band. I want to keep this band for a very long time and I want to be an integral part of it."

Thus the band is run on very democratic lines, and now the group are writing almost as much material as Kiki is herself.

"I'm not a prolific writer. I can't just sit down and turn out a string of songs to order. I suppose I'm what you might call a one-off writer."

Now the band are acquiring a reputation as a strong live outfit, prestige tours are getting easier to come by and interest in America is high.

Among fans Kiki already has something of a cult following, much like Melanie's, consisting of kids who crouch at the front of the stage pressing forward with gifts of flowers just to be near her.

Britain's never had a girl singer-songwriter in the Carole King mould before. All the signs are that Kiki's going to occupy that position before very long.

"We're in no hurry," she says with quiet confidence. "You can't force things, and it's of no help to be subjected to pressures. The music would only suffer and I wouldn't be happy about it."

Right now though, Kiki has every reason to be happy.

Queen

By Rosie Horide

EVEN THOSE who dislike the group intensely will concede that Queen's rise to fame in '74 has been meteoric. They first came to the attention of a large section of the public in the latter part of '73 when they supported Mott the Hoople on a large British tour.

"Mott were so good to us, giving us advice so that we didn't make as many mistakes as they had done when they were starting out," Brian May told me. And the concensus of opinion was that "we've never worked with anyone nicer."

"We decided we couldn't do any more support tours after that, it just wouldn't have been right for us." That was Freddie's comment after the tour. Their first album "Queen" had sold more than 30,000 copies already—an unheard of total for an "unknown" group.

It was already being predicted that the next album would reach at least the Top Ten in the album charts. What wasn't so easily forseeable was a hit single. With *"Seven Seas Of Rhye"* they had just that.

Queen were rehearsing in a studio in Ealing when the call came to tell them they were wanted for TV's Top Of The Pops. I'd gone down to have a sneak preview of their new stage act, and we were perched around a tiny dressing room sipping tea when the phone rang.

Were they delighted? Hardly. "I don't think we should do it," Freddie commented, prowling round the room gesticulating with his hands to substantiate his argument. "We don't want anyone to think we're just a singles band—they'll get totally the wrong impression," he concluded petulantly. Their main worry, apart from the group's image, was that they wouldn't be able to get the sound right in the few hours available to them.

The first thing you appreciate about Queen is that they are incredible perfectionists—even the best is often not good enough.

At 3 am on the day of the show they were still to be found in Pete Townshend's studios in Battersea. Eventually they got the sound as close as possible to the original, although they had no sleep that night.

That little story should serve to il-

lustrate a few points about Queen's collective character. It'll also give you some idea how long the "Queen II" album took to record!

Even then that album wasn't perfect to their minds—although a lot of people didn't agree with them, and the predictions of its success were proved to have been conservative.

So at the start of their very own British tour Queen had a hit single and an album. Despite the trials and tribulations of breakdowns and un-suitable venues, Queen emerged from that tour with a triumphant gig at the London Rainbow—just to prove to anyone who dared still doubt it that they'd arrived.

But as I sat in Freddie's Kensington flat the week after that Rainbow gig, they still had plenty of things they wanted to say.

First Freddie. "We're going to have to learn to think quicker, because I hate compromises—everything's got to be done to perfection. I think the public know how much work has gone into an album or any piece of music and appreciate it.

"That's why I get so furious when people say we aren't good musicians—they can criticise anything else about us, but I believe we are technically good, whether you like our music or not.

"The other criticisms we hate are when people say we're a hype—how can we be when it's taken four years for our music and act to evolve? Two years ago we were wearing similar clothes, and no one was backing us at all then—we didn't have a recording contract."

Freddie's favourite hobby horse, understandably enough. Two other things dear to his heart are clothes and his stage act: "I always want to look good—that's important to me. I hate off the peg clothes, and will spend weeks (when there's time) delving for bargains and unusual clothes.

"As for my stage act, of course I've seen and been influenced by other people on stage. But what I do on stage is all mine—something that's evolved naturally. Art and music have always gone hand in hand, and the theatrical side of music has always been important to me."

Brian also feels strongly about Queen and its critics. After all, when you've been playing guitar for as long as you can remember and even spent two years of your life building a guitar from scratch it's hard to be told you have no talent.

Brian, the most *obviously* talented member of the group musically (just listen to those astounding guitar breaks) would never denigrate the contribution made to the group by John Deacon and Roger Taylor—the self-styled rhythm section or "sonic volcano".

John never has a lot to say for himself, content to be a steadying influence on a group of opinionated and in many ways extrovert people. Roger smiles more often than anything else, but ventures an opinion readily when he feels strongly about something.

This then is Queen. Already they have done great things. They may do even greater. There is certainly still enormous undiscovered potential talent in those four people, both collectively and as a unit.

Queen: (left to right) Roger Taylor, Brian May, Freddie Mercury, John Deacon.

Alvin Stardust

SHANE Fenton was a quiet, normal sort of guy who lived in Knotty Ash, Liverpool, with his wife and children. Alvin Stardust is a mean, moody looking guy, always dressed in black, a pop star whose manner on stage is threatening to say the least.

Hard to believe they're the same man, isn't it? It just goes to show what a hit record can do.

After a successful career as a pre-Beatles pop star, 1973 found Shane Fenton making a living from occasional cabaret jobs in northern clubs. "Playing music was all I knew how to do, so I just carried on. It wasn't a bad life and we made a living."

But that peaceful existence wasn't to continue. A producer and writer called Peter Shelley had a number called, *"My Coo Ca Choo"* that needed someone to record it . . .

By Rosie Horide

Most of you know the story after that. A strange sight in pink and blue appeared on a TV pop programme, but as the record showed every sign of being a hit the image swiftly changed to the Alvin in black we all know and love.

"I've always worn black or dark blue, so it's normal for me," Shane/Alvin told me. "I did feel a bit silly in all that pink and blue stuff though. Still, they knew what they were doing, didn't they? It worked."

It certainly did. Suddenly everyone wanted to know about Alvin Stardust. It was only revealed to the general public that he had been Shane Fenton when a couple of eagle-eyed people thought they recognised him.

"It's amazing—I get recognised

everywhere," Alvin said. "Funny thing is that the young people recognize me as Alvin Stardust, and the older ones as Shane Fenton."

That's hardly surprising, for he hasn't changed facially since those early days when Shane Fenton had several big hit records. *"Five Foot Two, Eyes of Blue"* and *"Moody Guy"* were two of his successes.

Shane Fenton has now ceased to exist, for the time being anyway. "Even my little boy answers the 'phone and says 'hello, this is Shaun Stardust'. He's really knocked out with the whole thing."

As time has progressed and the Stardust hits have come and gone, Alvin has felt sure enough of his own position to resist some of the image-making which those around him have gone in for on his behalf. Within a year of the advent of Alvin as a per-

Alvin when he was Shane Fenton

sonality, the image had settled to a slightly larger than life version of the real man.

His stage achievements have been considerable—he settled back into the big time with no trouble at all, and soon had the fans screaming just like the good old days.

"I have been on the road for a few years," he'll tell you, grinning. "It's quite easy really. You fix your attention on one particular person—usually a girl!—and perform to her all the time. That way you really manage to communicate with the audience."

The fan worship astounds the modest lad. "I just happened to mention that I might turn up at a particular event, and they got a thousand more people there than was normal. After a couple of words they had to hustle me off when the kids rushed the stage. It was amazing."

Surprised though Alvin may be at getting a second chance of stardom, he's not going to let such an opportunity slip through his fingers again. When stardom came to Shane Fenton he was a kid in his teens who knew little or nothing about the music business. Alvin Stardust is a very different proposition.

"But I'm still learning. Don't forget, after all my years in the business it was only in 1974 I had my first ever album out! My producer Peter Shelley taught me things in the studio that I would never have believed possible—how a voice can be made to sound exactly the way you want it to. There was nothing like that in the days of *Moody Guy*."

The advent of Alvin's first album, "The Untouchable" also brought other facets of the Stardust talent to the fore.

"I wrote four of the tracks—it's very satisfying. They're mostly about people I've known and things that have happened to me or acquaintances."

No matter how famous he becomes as an artist (or a writer!) it's hard to imagine Alvin Stardust ever becoming as hard as he appears on stage. People who've met him personally have often been struck with the amazing difference between that hard image and the nice guy behind it.

Strange stories have been told about him not being allowed to smile on stage or in photographs, and other odd things. How much of that is true no-one (except Alvin) knows for sure. What we do know is that he's a nice friendly guy who's always got a kind word and a smile for people, who can't really take his drink and is generally a long way from being mean and moody.

So let's hope Shane Fenton and Alvin Stardust co-exist for a long time—together they could go a long way.

Mott

By Fox-Cumming

IT'S AMAZING how the fortunes of some bands can change. Take Mott The Hoople for example. A few years ago they'd split, embittered, saddened and disillusioned with the whole music business, and now they are on the crest of a wave talking about themselves in the same breath as The Beatles and The Stones.

You may think they are being a bit cheeky comparing themselves to the two bands who still tower in achievement over anything that has happened since, but the comparisons are not presumptious.

"These days," says Mott's front man Ian Hunter, "bands are divided into rock bands and pop groups. We think of ourselves as a rock band, which might lead you to think that we also consider ourselves as album artists rather than singles artists, and that is not the case.

"Very few bands have succeeded in being both singles and albums artists—both The Beatles and The Stones did, and we'd like to be able to tread the same line, although I know it's precarious.

"But if people began to think of us more in the singles vein and started discounting our albums, then I'd

think very seriously about not putting out any more singles."

Mott have now reached the position both here and in the States, where they are much bigger for example than either Slade or Bolan, that they can call the tune on most things. They don't have to make records they don't want to; they don't have to accept second billing on tours that really are not to their liking. But it wasn't always that way.

In the early days they were often accused of being too Dylan-influenced, and also of being the puppets of their producer Guy Stevens. People less kindly disposed towards them simply wrote them off as all noise and no music. They did have a following though, so strong that they were almost a cult band.

In the end, however, Mott could see that they'd reached the limit. The solid knot of fans they'd accumulated would stay with them forever, but would not get appreciably bigger, and they were covering the same old ground over and over again. So, suddenly, in Switzerland, they split and embarked on a round of parties to

drown their sorrows and make whoopee.

As everyone now knows, it was David Bowie who rescued the band by insisting they got into a recording studio just one more time and furnishing them with a classic best-selling single "All The Young Dudes" and a hit album with the same title.

But then, inevitably, Mott got put down as Bowie satellites and were given little credit for their part in the proceedings. In the end they simply *had* to write a hit single for themselves. With "Honaloochie Boogie" they succeeded, and since then they've never looked back. The confidence that gave them not only manifested itself in their ensuing albums, but also in their stage performances.

Suddenly a band that had always been at the best, erratic, settled down to produce consistently thrilling concerts. They found not only a whole new broad-based audience, but also began to make a number of friends among rock critics.

Now having succeeded in eliminating a glaringly red bank balance, they have been able to increase their personnel and Ariel Bender and Morgan Fisher in particular have brought new life to the band's stage work.

Ian Hunter is ecstatic about his band now more than ever before. "I'm a great front man now," he boasts, "because I know I have a great band behind me.

"Mott takes up all my time. I hear very few records of other people's these days. I mean, I haven't even heard The Stones' latest album. Also if you avoid hearing other people's work, you avoid it getting into your subconscious so that later it filters into your own stuff.

"People have begun to say that I'm an ogre in this band, that my songs take precedence over any the rest of the band provide.

"That isn't the case at all. I write songs and take them to the band. They are the jury, if the stuff I write isn't good enough, they'll tell me so.

"I want to make it very clear that I don't run this band. Buffin (Mott's drummer) for instance has a lot more to do with the production of our albums these days than I do."

If you talk to any of the rest of the band, they all seem more than happy with the way things are going for them, so one can take it as gospel that

Mott is in fact a democratic outfit.

For an interesting picture of a band still on its way to the top, you should read Ian's book "Diary Of A Rock 'n' Roll Star". If you haven't already read it, you be ashamed of yourself, since for any rock fan, be they a Mott lover or not, it's nigh on essential reading.

Ian viewed the book as an exercise in self-discipline. "I found I was getting a bit sloppy in my approach to our work at the time. I needed to sit down and make myself do something like that.

"I doubt if I'll ever write another book like it, though maybe one day I'd like to write a book of verse. Seems a bit silly though somehow."

Perhaps that last remark contains part of the secret of Mott's success. They've gone out of their way to keep with their fans, and never try anything that might seem aimed above people's heads.

As Ian says: "My consumer is a teenager around 15 years old. To reach him, I have to be his spokesman and to do that I have to think like him.

"People say we're temperamental and difficult to deal with, but if I'm to relate to my audience I have to be like them. A fifteen year old has a rebellious streak, has tantrums, and I must be the same. We all must."

Overend Watts

Mud

By Rosie Horide

EARLY IN 1974 at a gig in the Brighton Dome, one of Mud's roadies leaned over and said to me: "These guys are going to be the biggest thing in the country by the end of the year."

Now we can look back and see how close they came to fulfilling his prophesy. It was certainly a good year.

1974 began for Mud with the release of a single called *"Tiger Feet"*. As always with a new single, the boys were worried about it.

"I don't think it's as strong as *'Dyna-Mite'*," drummer and spokesman Dave Mount confided in me at the time. But with typical dedication they worked out a closely choreographed routine, complete with a brand new set of costumes.

The red drape jackets and drainpipe trousers were carefully chosen to complement the dancing—an extension of a dance the boys had watched the audience doing to their numbers.

"We have to learn from them, it makes sense doesn't it? That way we give them what we want." Front man Les Gray, being his usual down-to-earth self.

The first time I saw Mud perform *"Tiger Feet"* was at Hastings Pier Pavilion on Christmas Eve. It went down incredibly well for a new number. The predominantly "rocker" audience loved it.

The following month that song gave the group their first number one. Even people whose life is pop music were seen to bop around to it, and Mud's pleasure was a delight to see.

"We've made it, after all these years. I can't believe it." Dave said that, but they all felt it. "Five years or more playing all those gigs all round the country. Then all those records—some complete flops, the more recent ones very nearly making it. And now we're really number one."

That particular night at Top of the Pops, Sweet were also on the show. Understandably enough, they were a little upset. Any murmurs of consolation at their only being at number two received very short shrift.

The rivalry (although Mud insisted there wasn't really any on their part) was also natural. Both bands had material written for them by the phenomenally successful Chinn and Chapman, and whoever lost the battle was bound to believe they'd been given the inferior song.

Yet Mud had progressed from being a "second string" group to one of Chinnichap's most successful. For several months special songs taking their definite talents into consideration had been the order of the day.

Ironically, Sweet and Chinnichap now have little to do with each other. Some matters were so controversial that in the end it must have been hard to continue the partnership. Eventually the "nice guys" won.

At times being nice can't have been easy. "People haven't always been nice to *us*," says Dave. "There were several times when people dismissed us as just another singles band—a hype."

In fact Mud have worked very hard to get where they are today. Even when they had the first hits all their commitments were fulfilled. And in the meantime their individual personalities have become more apparent, both on and off stage.

Dave Mount is the spokesman, the organiser. One of the more talkative members of the group, on stage Dave's mode of expression is his drumming. Recently the rest of the boys have played up his "underprivileged" position as the man in the background on stage, which nobody—especially Dave—really believes.

Rob is the quietest member of the group—a word of praise will bring a coy smile to his face, but a conversation of any length is unlikely unless he's known you for some time.

He's always the one to wear the more effeminate clothes: "I always get lumbered with the frilly things" he'll tell you. "He's not really the butch type though, is he." Les points out.

Rob is also a very talented musician. The happiest I've ever seen him look is the day he heard he'd passed the top grade exam in classical guitar. What was that about Mud not being musicians?

Lead guitarist Ray is also quiet off stage—but in front of an audience his character changes. He woos the audience with his guitar, smiling all the while, and playing the sort of riffs some of our most respected guitarists would be proud to own.

Ray was the first to be dragged off stage by over-enthusiastic fans, but accepted it all with his usual calm.

Last but not least we come to Les Gray. Front man and lead vocalist, he's the group's extrovert. Les throws himself with abandon into the dressing up and dance routines, embellishing them with his own little touches.

The monster comb that comes out to slick back the DA haircut is one example. "It's all good fun, isn't it." That's Les's philosophy. "We like to think of ourselves as entertainers as well as musicians, and that means everyone enjoying themselves: us and the audiences."

As 1974 has progressed they've been so successful as entertainers and musicians that they've gained a well-deserved reputation as a fine live group. At each gig they gain a few more fans, and a thousand outside the dressing room is quite normal. Being mobbed is a very real threat to them.

I think the roadie wasn't far from being right: look to your laurels Slade and Gary. Mud are challenging your position with their fine live act and singles success. Their album proved they are not to be trifled with musically—Mud, a group to be reckoned with.

MUD—Rob Davis at back and left to right front, Dave Mount, Ray Stiles and Les Gray.

Roy Wood

By Rosie Horide

"I WOULDN'T call myself a musician." Right. Any guesses which pop luminary uttered those words? Would you believe Roy Wood?

"I'm more a composer who does things . . . I suppose I do play a lot of instruments. I'm not technically good at each one, I play in my own way, which is pretty unauthentic. I don't play the oboe or the cello the way a real oboist or cellist would, but I still get the sound I want out of it.

"I'm not able to write in music form. I don't write music at all. I have my own code for writing things down, although hardly anyone else can understand it. But when I want to explain something to the others I usually play it to them and they pick it up from there."

The words of a man who can take the credit for more hits than he cares to remember in the past ten years, and who was voted Top Musician by the readers of Disc. His reaction to the award was typically honest: "They must be mad."

In fact many of those people would probably credit him with more than just Top Musician—in pop terms he's often considered to be a genius! When you think of the ideas he's originated during his involvement with the Move, ELO and Wizzard it's hardly surprising. In fact you never know what he's going to come up with next: like the *"Highland Reggae"*!

That craze began with the release of Roy's solo single *"Going Down The*

Rick Price—Wizzard organiser and friend

Road". Not only was it a highland reggae complete with bagpipes, but had "backing vocals" from sheep and cows!

"I think a songwriter needs to get into as many fields as he possibly can—then if one thing goes out of fashion, he has the others to fall back on. That's why I'm always trying out new things."

With sheep and cows, Roy certainly got into different "fields". (Oops, sorry about that.) Whether you like his music or not, no-one can ever say Roy's records are boring or repetitive.

One that was a hit in the summer of 1974 caused a certain amount of controversy:

"It was due to come out in January, and a lot of people slagged me off for releasing it when the sun was out. After all it was called Rock 'n' Roll Winter!

"I did consider saving it until the following winter, but for all I knew Wizzard might be into something completely different by them so I decided to put it out anyway."

Cirticisms or not, that single was a big hit and Roy was able to go on to even bigger things. Looking back on the year, his greatest success was improving Wizzard's stage act so that they became acceptable to their record-buying audience on stage too.

The idea was "trying to make the act sound a lot more like the Wizzard singles, because that's what the kids want to hear." From the reviews, and what we saw, he was very successful.

But one things didn't work as well as he'd hoped: the girl vocalists which Wizzard took on tour with them.

"The girls help to get the Spector sound better—singles just didn't sound the same without the female voices. But taking the girls on tour didn't really work out—there were a lot of problems we hadn't forseen, even silly little things like extra dressing room facilities we needed, that made it all more trouble than it was worth."

Never mind. As Roy said at the time, you can't win 'em all. He does manage to win more than most. This year he even got an Ivor Novello award, which he was really chuffed about.

"I did a little dance round the house when I found out," he said grinning, and looking more like a pixie than a wizzard. "It's really great."

Amazing to think that until fairly recently Roy didn't even have a silver disc to his credit; that after all those years of hits with the Move (including a number one with "Blackberry Way") Roy had to wait 'til the first Wizzard single "Ball Park Incident" for his first ever silver disc. Since then they've been coming thick and fast.

Once Roy has his studio built at the house, there'll be no stopping him.

"You see, I'm nocturnal person really. I can only work and write at night time. If I had the studio at the house I could fall out of bed and straight into the studio . . . then back into bed when I was tired."

"There are a lot of different things I've not had time to work on yet. I won't tell you about them, I want them to be a surprise."

There's little doubt they'll be that, Roy. And don't be surprised if green/tartan hair and all, you find yourself voted top musician again by the mad Disc readers who love you for the fun you've brought back into music.

Medicine Head: John Fiddler, Peter Hope-Evans (far right)

Medic Head

Peter Hope-Evans

By Andy Blackford

"WE'LL always stay as a two-piece band. Peter and I are self-sufficient. We don't need anybody else." Thus spake John Fiddler in an interview with Disc in 1973. And yet within a matter of two months, a five piece Medicine Head was touring the country.

What was the reason behind this sudden change of heart? "It was down to the hit records, really," explains John. "We'd always vowed we wouldn't add permanent members to the group; as far as we were con-cerned, it was Peter and myself, perhaps with occasional back-up musicians for particular gigs.

"But we found we were becoming increasingly schizophrenic. Our old fans expected us to play as a duo, but there were huge numbers of new followers who only knew us through *'One and One'* and *'Rising Sun'*. They expected us to recreate the sound of the records.

"We could get a big sound in the studio, using overdubs and double tracking. But on stage it was difficult.

"When we first added the other musicians, we didn't regard them as a permanent part of the band. But we found we were so suited to one another that we couldn't do without them."

The first new member was guitarist Roger Saunders. "I'd never met the guy, but I'd heard some of his songs because we shared the same management. I wasn't too interested in his band, Freedom—they were a heavy three-piece. But he'd made a couple of solo albums and I liked the way he went about things.

"He's a good piano player, too. Now that we've got over the panic of trying to get a stage-act together in a rush, we plan to develop his talents more fully.

"I play keyboards, too, and I'd like to do some duets with him. Perhaps we'll be the new Alan Price and Georgie Fame . . ."

The bass player is George Ford, brother of singer Emile Ford. "At first I was angling for Pat Donaldson who played with Maggie Bell. But that fell through and George just appeared. He used to play with Linda Lewis in Ferris Wheel. When we found him, he was with the Roy Young Band."

Drummer Rob Townshend was looking for work after Family split up, and contacted John through their mutual friend, Tony Ashton. So the new, improved Medicine Head was complete.

If you've seen them, you must have been struck by the way Peter Hope-Evans stays in the background. In a group of five, he's even less conspicuous than he was as half of a two-piece.

He never speaks on stage. He doesn't sing. He doesn't write the material. So why does John attach so much importance to his contribution?

"Well, he's a great harp player."
But so's John, come to that.

"No—I mean, Peter's *really* good. He's got incredible power. And his style's unique. But most of all, he's a 'presence'?

"I think he's got an incredibly powerful stage image. He doesn't have to say anything. He just stands there. I see him as a vital part of the group's atmoshere.

"I've known him since 1964, and I've seen all his changes. You'd never guess it, but he used to be really 'loud'.

"But when he got kicked out of college he had a tough year, and it changed him completely. He had to do all sorts of stupid jobs, just to survive. He had a bad scene with a chick, too. He wanted to marry her, and all that.

"Then his mates introduced him to the Meher Baba mystical thing—Eastern religion—and the next time I saw him he was a recluse."

I'd toyed with the idea of interviewing Peter instead of John, just because I've never seen a convincing article about him. But John soon persuaded me it would've been a Herculean task.

"He once did an interview for a rock magazine, and he didn't say a word for an hour. The reporter was tearing his hair out. Then he spoke. 'I'd like you to leave the page completely blank,' he said. And they did. The magazine appeared with a big; white space. Underneath it said, 'This space was donated by Peter Hope-Evans. Fill it with whatever you like.'

"That's the area of communication that he's into at the moment. It makes him seem aloof and unapproachable if you don't know him.

"But in fact, he's a tremendously warm person.

"He's amazingly generous, too. He seems to give away the things he loves most. Our first album, for instance. I'd never have parted with my copy—I hung on to it for all the wrong reasons, I suppose. Just because *I* wanted it.

"But Peter gave his away. He's only just managed to get hold of another copy—picked it up in a junk shop."

There's something contradictory about a mystic and recluse being a member of a pop group, and John confesses that it puzzles him, too.

"I guess I don't know him, even after all this time. In his private life he's so quiet and introverted. I don't know what makes him put on a white suit and a hat and pushes him on to a stage in front of hundreds of people. It's a mystery.

"He has a highly original approach to playing in a group. Like he has this box-file he calls his 'studio survival kit'. He keeps loads of magazines in it—a roll of sticky tape and pair of scissors. When he's not actually recording, he cuts up the magazines and sticks them back together so they make his kind of sense.

"And he'll rearrange hotel rooms—move the furniture about—even if he's only going to be there for the night. He'll do additional artwork on those awful pictures you get in hotels, too. He likes to alter the universe, to impose his own ideas upon it."

Although Peter doesn't write lyrics for Medicine Head, he writes a lot of poetry, and has had a book of his work published.

"He's written so much lately, it's time we did something with it. We've got plans to produce an album of his poetry soon. I don't know whether I'll be putting the poems to music or not. If there is music, it'll be mostly percussion. Peter's in to primitive instruments—drums, bells, mouthbows.

"One thing's for certain—it won't sound anything like Medicine Head."

Kung Fu

WHAT goes with pop like cream goes with strawberries? It used to be Meditation in the heyday of the Beatles, and it carried over into the flower power days.

Today the fad still comes from the East—not so peaceful, but just as demanding to the addicted. It is Kung Fu the ancient oriental art of self defence.

The martial arts are taking over as the box office successes in the cinema—spearheaded by the late Bruce Lee who died just as he was approching the pinnacle of his success.

Then David Carradine grabs the TV ratings with his hippy half breed as he wanders the old West with peace, understanding, and a swift foot in the mouth for those who push him too far.

Here we ask Carradine about himself and Kung Fu—and a few of today's top stars for their views.

DAVID CARRADINE

SO THIS is the studio back-lot that gave the world James Dean? And Humphrey Bogart. And Paul Newman.

Now the same, seedy, two-dimensional Western streets are walked barefoot by a new star. Studio executives at Warner Brothers in beautiful downtown Burbank call him: "Our hippie Star."

"Aw come on man, I'm not even a beatnik," says David Carradine, the most unlikely £4,000-a-week man in captivity.

He is Caine, the half-Chinese hero of the Kung Fu TV series.

He spends a lot of time telling people how normal he is. Somehow it never sounds convincing.

"I'm just a working jerk right," he said wearily. "And I whistle while I'm doing it.

"I'm an actor, just doing what my daddy did."

Daddy is Hollywood actor John Carradine. Remember him as the doctor in John Ford's classic Stagecoach?

Carradine senior is tall, greying, distinguished. A doyen of Hollywood.

Carradine junior has never fitted in. As a child he ran away from home with monotonous regularity. He shop-lifted liberally.

Now at 37 he is living with a woman who is not his wife—actress Barbara Hershey—and their child. My god, the man doesn't even have a swimming pool. When he wants to swim he uses the Pacific. Regular folk are scandalised.

It took four hours to get Carradine to talk in something more than grunts. When he finally gave way it poured out in a never-ending stream.

He said: "I did a screen test for a Kung Fu movie.

"When I walked into that room with a shaved head and bare feet the producers flipped.

"I knew I was ready for this part. I'd been waiting for this part all my life without knowing what it was.

"I read the Kung Fu script and I knew. I knew this was the Arrivals Terminal, yer dig? Like here I take off.

"There wasn't an actor in America, maybe not in the whole world, who was as fitted as me to do this part."

Carradine knows nothing about the practice of Kung Fu. When the rather ordinary film was turned into an extraordinary TV series he faced the problem of a weekly Kung Fu fight.

He uses his training as a dancer to work them out. But if he was attacked in a bar—as has happened—he would be beaten by one blow to the jaw—as has happened.

"I am NOT, repeat in big capital letters NOT, into the fight scene," said Carradine.

"What I am into is trying to see inside life, to take life as it comes and react to it.

"One day I am going to blast off into hyper-space and sit on top of a celestial mountain and look down and see what it's all been about.

"I don't own a TV. I play the guitar but what I play doesn't matter. It's something to do with my hands while I'm contemplating the Cosmos.

"I make movies with my friends. That's where all my money goes apart from cars.

"It doesn't matter what they are about. It's the way they are made. So long as there is a process different to the commercial Hollywood process then everything's OK. There's hope left.

"That's what Kung Fu gives. Hope. That and the frame of mind to just think, contemplate, be aware."

It sounds arrogant. In the flesh it drops from the lips of a smiling, courteous man. He hates explaining anything. This is hard work for David Carradine.

"I know I'm not arrogant. I don't have a big head. It always comes out that way on paper and that's a drag.

"But it's not me. I am proud, I agree to that. I am a very proud man but I am no Messiah, no John The Baptist.

"I feel that I am a religious being but it is religion working through me to reach people. I don't create anything.

"I am like an instrument and I just let the Universe blow me."

What are the stars' views on Kung Fu? On the next few pages we find out

GARY GLITTER

"I'M THE GREATEST fan of the Kung Fu TV series this side of the Great Wall of China.

"Hate that violence—I think it's unnecessary. But I love the show because it's essentially non-violent. David Carradine never thumps the baddies for the sake of it. Kung Fu is always a last resort—true self-defence.

"But the reason I like it most is because of the religion in it. It's just like the Bible, but hip. Religion shouldn't be heavy—it should be fun.

I don't practise any martial arts myself, but I can stick up for myself in a bundle. I did some boxing at school and I'm pretty quick on my feet. In fact, I've got my own fail-safe technique for winning fights. If someone's messing me about, I say, 'I'm going to count up to three, and if you haven't packed it in, I'm going to lay one on you'. Then I count up to two and lay one on him. It's fool-proof . . ."

In Gary's film, "Remember Me This Way", he is seen performing super-human feats of Carradine/Lee-like athletics.

"I'm supposed to be doing a screen-test. I'm on the phone to a bird, and I tell her I'll be over in about twenty minutes. Then three ominous shadows fall over the table and I just say, 'Hey, make that thirty.' Then these guys come bursting in and I've got to deal with them.

"I knock one of their heads through a table. In the rehearsal we used a stunt man and a balsa wood table. I bashed his face down on to the surface and as planned, it went straight through. But he didn't get up again. He was unconscious, I'd broken his nose. Stunt men have this professional pride thing about not getting injured, and when he finally came round, he stood there with tears of pain streaming down his cheeks. 'Don't worry,' he kept saying, 'I'm fine. Just fine.'

"Next I had to chuck one of them through a window. The poor guy had to go through it three times before I got it right."

ALVIN STARDUST

MUD'S LES GRAY

"ONE OF our roadies is a Kung Fu expert. He's just had a nasty accident as a result of it. He got kicked below the belt and was off for four weeks. As for the group we have nothing to do with it. As long as John, our roadie, can keep an eye on us that's OK. Knowing the agony he went through in hospital for a fortnight after his accident I don't think any of us would want to go in for it.

"The truth is we avoid all trouble. It's very rare we have any. Of course, John isn't allowed to use Kung Fu except in self-defence. He had to sign a vow agreeing to that. If he attacked somebody without real cause he would be fined heavily."

DAVID ESSEX

"THE TV show knocks me out. Maybe it's a bad influence if it makes kids grab each other. My four-year-old son sometimes leaps on my back and shouts Kung Fu. But I guess kids emulate whatever is going on. Violence has always been popular—stoneage kids probably threw rocks like their fathers did, so it's hard to judge how bad it is.

"I've been a member of so many Judo and Karate clubs, I can hardly remember. One in Liverpool, one in Barcelona, one in Paris, two in London—but I never stick to the course, so I can't remember much. I'm not a fighter, by any means, but if it looks like you're going to get hurt, you have to defend yourself. One of my best friends was a calm, respected gentleman by nature . . . later, I found out he was a karate instructor.

"You'll find the instructors at these courses will ask you why you've come—and if it's to learn to fight . . . goodnight. It's a mental exercise; a sport. I don't have any trouble with aggressive people—I have a masculine image and a sex image which seems to please the girls and the guys. Basically, though, I'm pretty docile. You have to be serious if you're going for Kung Fu. It's a young man's game of golf."

"I ONCE did judo some years ago, but I don't really know anything about Kung Fu. To be honest I'm not really interested. I know it's big in America and a lot of kids watch the programme on TV, but as far as I'm concerned it's just a passing craze.

"Why these things never really work out is because you've got to have complete dedication. It takes 10 years to master it and by that time most people would have tired of it."

MEDICINE HEAD'S JOHN FIDDLER

IAN HUNTER

"I LIKE David Carradine—he's always been a bit of a lad. On Kung Fu, I don't know much about it . . . but I don't think I could devote my life to something like that—or gardening, either. When I was younger, I'd get approached in bars, like everybody else. I'd just grab them by the neck and hope for the best! Now, I get approached by different sorts in bars! I haven't got any reason to leap six feet in the air and kick somebody. As for the fans who rush the stage, we have something to deal with that; it's called Roadie Fu—but it doesn't hurt."

ALICE COOPER

"I'M a pacifist but that doesn't mean I'm totally against violence. It's just that I'd always try a peaceful way out before resorting to physical means of solving an argument.

"I don't know any obscure and wonderful ways of defending myself. I rely on the old one-two.

"As for the Kung Fu series, I enjoy it a lot. Unlike Peter (Hope-Evans) I've never really been into Oriental philosophy and meditation, but I can appreciate all the wise sayings, et cetera. Like, 'Ah, Grasshopper, love is like a many-speckled toad leaping through the long grass of a Saturday afternoon'.

"But mostly I dig it simply on the entertainment level. It's fun."

"I'M the most gentle man in the world—off stage," I hate violence of any sort. But I love TV. People want to know why my stage act is so violent. I'll tell you why. Americans have got no culture (Actually they have, but it's only three hundred years old). So we get by on television culture which is just sex and violence. That's fine—I could sit and watch sex and violence all night.

'I dig the Kung Fu series. It's great. But then, I dig anything so long as the picture's good.

"I don't practise any form of self defense myself. I never get angry enough. I *am* doing a spot of fencing lately, but it's only a sport as far as I'm concerned. I couldn't foresee myself running anybody through with my rapier."

Bruce Lee